Praise for
Dreamguider

If I were back in the fourth grade, I might just decide to spend my pocket money buying my parents a copy of Denyse Beaudet's book, because it says so many cool things kids need adults to know about dreams. One is that children know more about dreaming than most adults, so grown-ups should make a space to listen up. They should help kids to record their dreams in journals that will be a gift to the family decades later. If a kid is scared by something in the night, parents need to be primed to help, by offering immediate comfort, by checking whether the dream offers a clue to a problem that needs to be addressed, and sometimes by assisting the child to "continue" the dream until a terror is confronted and resolved. The section on helping kids to select a dream talisman or night guardian is alone worth the price of the book, and I *know* it works. Clear, practical, and warm-hearted, alive with the voices of dreaming children, *Dreamguider* offers essential education for parents everywhere.

—Robert Moss, author of *Conscious Dreaming*
and *The Three "Only" Things: Tapping
the Power of Dreams, Coincidence,
and Imagination*

Also by Denyse Beaudet

_____

Encountering the Monster:
Pathways in Children's Dreams

DREAMGUIDER

Open the Door to Your Child's Dreams

DENYSE BEAUDET, PHD

HAMPTON ROADS
PUBLISHING COMPANY, INC.

Cover design by Kathryn Sky-Peck
Cover art: *Little Boy Asleep in Bed Dreaming*
by Charles Settrington, Stone/Getty Images

Hampton Roads Publishing Company, Inc.
1125 Stoney Ridge Road
Charlottesville, VA 22902

434-296-2772
fax: 434-296-5096
e-mail: hrpc@hrpub.com
www.hrpub.com

If you are unable to order this book from your local
bookseller, you may order directly from the publisher.
Call 1-800-766-8009, toll-free.

Library of Congress Cataloging-in-Publication Data

Beaudet, Denyse.
Dreamguider : open the door to your child's dreams / Denyse Beaudet.
    p. cm.
Includes bibliographical references and index.
Summary: "A guide for parents into the world of their children's dreams,
which often reveal their thoughts, feelings, and imaginations. Parents learn
how to help children understand and not fear their dreams"--Provided by
publisher.

ISBN 978-1-57174-593-4 (alk. paper)
1. Children's dreams. 2. Parenting. 3. Child rearing. I. Title.
BF1099.C55B425 2008
154.6'3083--dc22
                                    2008036605

ISBN 978-1-57174-593-4
10 9 8 7 6 5 4 3 2 1
Printed on acid-free paper in the United States

DEDICATION

To my Father and to my Mother

CONTENTS

Acknowledgments

Numerous benevolent allies have come my way to make the publication of *Dreamguider* a reality. Each one of them has contributed his or her unique talent. To each one of them I am deeply grateful. My agent, Dena Fisher, from Manus & Associates Literary Agency, thought to herself, "I want to do this with my kids," as she first read the proposal for *Dreamguider.* Her responsiveness and professionalism have been unwavering. It is my pleasure to know her and to work with her.

My editor, Tershia d'Elgin, captured the essence of her art when she told me, "I'm a book doctor." Tershia put the best of her talents to work as communicator and editor in serving *Dreamguider* and in making its message accessible. Her efforts to attune herself to the deepest intentions of my text have been remarkable; her help with reframing meanings in the American language, invaluable. Whenever I think of someone who has been a creative contributor to this project, I think of her kind and humor-laden sensibilities. What a difference she has made!

My heartfelt gratitude goes to Jack Jennings, CEO of Hampton Roads, for publishing *Dreamguider* for its unique approach to children's dreams. Several professionals at Hampton Roads have added their touch to the production of *Dreamguider.* Kathryn Sky-Peck brought vision and art to her cover-design. The result is not only strikingly beautiful, it is evocative of the magic of opening a door to a child's world of dreams. Margaret Smith's layout design adds a dimension to the text; through images and the use of space, she conveys both a poetic sense and clarity. Production editor Tania Seymour provided attentive content editing and copy editing. Tania lighted the way for me through the production process. I thank her as well as Kathryn Sky-Peck and Margaret Smith. I also want to acknowledge Jane Hagaman (Production/Art Director), Sara Sgarlat (Publicity Director), and Greg Brandenburgh (Sales/Marketing Director) for their availability, guidance, and enthusiasm for the diffusion of *Dreamguider.*

A *dreamguider* is a *guider* for *dreams* and for *dreaming* from the point of view of a child. My daughter Mikhaëla gave the name to me for my e-mail address when she was twelve. Writing for parents about guiding children in the art of dreaming, I adopted the name for the book title. I thank Mikhaëla for coining the phrase that became my book title.

My husband David has been a longtime ally to *Dreamguider.* As parents, both of us took part in the recording of our daughter's dreams. His education as an English major at UCLA, his work as a poet, and his training as a psychologist have benefited this project. He has provided keen editing and psychological insights. David has groused and grimaced and smiled his way through many ultra-intense periods for the sake of the dreams of

children. I feel an endless gratitude for his companion-
ship and his contributions to *Dreamguider.*

There is one more person to acknowledge: At a conference of the International Association for the Study of
Dreams in Berkeley some years ago, a man named Ralf
from the Gaia Book Store, looking at my first book, said
to me, "Go home and write another book and don't take
more than a year." Upon returning home from Berkeley,
I started writing. It took much more than one year for
Dreamguider to see the light of day. Yet through his words,
I recognized the moment. I thank him, wherever he may
be, for being a messenger for *Dreamguider.*

Dreams from children of all ages illustrate the ideas
presented in *Dreamguider.* Children, parents, and occasionally adults remembering childhood dreams have
shared these dreams with me. At times, I also drew from
other researchers and authors. I am grateful for all the
children's dreams that are contained in this book. I am
grateful to each of the children (research subjects, students, acquaintances, or family members) who shared
their dream lives and their dreams with me. I also thank
their parents for their kindness in authorizing their children to share dreams with me.

William A. Harris, now a professor at the University
of Cambridge, generously handed me the dream journal
he kept for his children. His recordings over several
years have provided precious data for my research and
for this work. Sarah Patee provided the dream journal

her seven-year-old had kept. Other parents shared their children's dreams. I thank Professor Harris, Sarah Patee, and each of the other parents for their gracious contributions to *Dreamguider.* I also thank the adults who shared with me their childhood dreams, and the parents who shared bedtime-ritual memories.

Jonie Nowatzki, director of the International Cooperative Nursery School at the University of California, San Diego, welcomed me to interview children on their beliefs about dreams. I thank Jonie Nowatzki, the teachers at ICNS, the children, and their parents for kindly allowing the children to participate in the interviews. I also want to acknowledge the participants in my interviews on children's beliefs about dreams from my earlier research, which never made into my first book and from which I also drew for *Dreamguider.*

In addition to selecting dreams for their illustrative properties, I strove to include dreams from young dreamers (up to age seven) and dreams from older dreamers (seven to fourteen) of both genders. Certain names and biographical details needed to be changed for the sake of confidentiality. In the end, I changed the names of all the children in order to treat everyone the same way. The dreamers will recognize themselves. Their dreams will be a gift to all those who will read them.

INTRODUCTION

For Westerners, a door to children's dreams first blew open in the 1930s with observations of the Malaysian Senoi. It has taken decades, however, for our families to step through that door. There are numerous reasons for this lag, beginning with profound cultural differences.

Unlike most parents in developed countries, the Senoi regard a child's dreams as a learning opportunity. They believe dreams school us in the art of life. Radically, the Senoi advise a child never to be afraid in a dream. If a child dreams of falling, the Senoi adult exclaims: "Magnificent! This is the most beautiful dream that you could ever have. Where did you fall? What have you discovered?" If the child awakens in fear before arriving anywhere, the adult says, "This is an error. Falling is the quickest way to get in touch with the world of spirits. Next time, surrender to the movement of falling and enjoy it." After a while, the adult knows, the child's fear of falling will change into the joy of flying.[1]

Continue a dream until it reaches a point of resolution, the Senoi counsel. Within a dream, they instruct, a child must act responsibly toward friends and other recognizable people. The Senoi also guide a child to move *toward* a dream tiger instead of away from it. They believe that a dream enemy will continue to pursue a child dreamer until the child has conquered it. Once conquered or befriended, a dream enemy will become the child's ally in the spirit world and in future dreams.[2]

Encountering and growing toward this wisdom, indicated the report on the Senoi, was part of every Senoi's upbringing. The Senoi approach, which I read about thirty years ago in an article by anthropologist Kilton Stewart, seemed revolutionary.[3] In the West, we commonly teach our children how to behave in waking reality. However, few think to guide their children in their dreaming. This news was as fresh as the rain forest from which it came!

In the West, dreams had been left in the dark for centuries. Our first attempts to reclaim dreams through psychoanalysis at the beginning of the twentieth century associated dreams with pathology. Little did we know that a small group of people from the other side of the globe possessed a secret. And the secret was not that dreams reflect illness, but that they are a sign of an innate drive to connect with oneself, with others, with nature, and with spirit.

Inspired by the Senoi, my study of children's dreams began. "How were children in the West, who were not taught 'the art of dreaming,' dealing with the wolves, witches, and monsters of their dreams?" This question engaged me in a ten-year study of the dreams of children and their ways of encountering the dream monster. It led to the publication of my first book, *Encountering the Monster: Pathways in Children's Dreams.*[4]

I found that dreams carry children, like the heroes of

myths and fairy tales, into adventures. Children went to a mountain, a forest, or an ocean and there encountered a monster. Sometimes children were called to an adventure by the monster intruding into the family dwelling. The first response was usually to refuse the call. In the dream, children cried, called for help, or escaped. Eventually, children took up the challenge raised by the monster, either alone or with the help of an ally. Their encounter took up to three pathways: combat, taming (or befriending), and engulfment.

Western children, my research suggested, were not devoid of art in their dream practice, as might have been expected, even though they had received no training in the art of dreaming. They had a kind of native ability as dreamers that called for more attention and respect.

When Kilton Stewart originally went to Malaysia in 1934, it was to join the research team of British anthropologist Herbert (Pat) Noone, who first discovered the dream people in the early thirties. At the time Noone came into contact with the Senoi, they lived in a thick and luxuriant jungle and they had never seen the ocean. The Senoi existed in harmony with nature and with their neighbors. Noone was taken with Senoi amiability and he attributed the Senoi peaceful way of life to their way of working with dreams.[5]

Other scientists followed. Then the war broke out, and during the Japanese occupation of Malaysia, the British took refuge in the jungle. Communist Chinese guerillas were also hiding in the jungle. The Senoi first served the British cause and later the cause of the Chinese Communists. The Senoi had a profound knowledge of the jungle, which made them invaluable allies for any group forced to withdraw to this unfamiliar territory. By the end of the war in 1945, liberation gradually returned the jungle to the Senoi and the government put medical and educational services at their disposal.[6]

The article by Kilton Stewart, "Dream Theory in Malaya," which brought the Senoi to the West's attention, was first published in 1951. In it, the tale of the dream people came through lucidly, with the appeal of a return to the source. When Stewart's article was reprinted in Charles Tart's *Altered States of Consciousness* in 1969, it caught the popular imagination.[7] Both Kilton Stewart and, after him, Patricia Garfield, in her book *Creative Dreaming* (published in 1974), described the Senoi as free from violence and mental illness as we know it.[8,9]

Yet, in his well-researched book, *The Mystique of Dreams: A Search for Utopia through Senoi Dream Theory,* G. William Domhoff challenged these claims. Reviewing the works of American anthropologists who had sojourned among the Senoi in the sixties and seventies, Domhoff provided contrasting facts and concluded "that Senoi psychology is more complex and typically human than the impression conveyed by Stewart and Garfield."[10] By then, of course, more than three decades, World War II, and lots of exposure to Westerners had intervened.

Travelers to Malaysia in search of the "dream people" were thus not finding what they had been led to expect in the Senoi.[11] By the time this more critical view of the Senoi began to emerge in the eighties, there were dream practitioners who had been following the Senoi principles for a few decades already and they knew that there was real gold in the Senoi way of dream education.

At the 1993 annual conference of the Association for

the Study of Dreams in Santa Fe, New Mexico, anthropologist and musicologist Marina Roseman, who had been conducting research with the Senoi for twelve years, brought fresh images and sounds from the dream people. Roseman reminded her audience that Senoi perceive the world around them as ensouled. The Senoi revere the spirits that animate the trees, the rivers, and the mountains. These spirits manifest in dreams. When gifted by an encounter with a spirit in a dream, the Senoi receive the dream with due reverence and honor the dream by implementing in their life what they have received from the dream.[12]

The Senoi continue to fascinate. Books are published and films produced about the Senoi.[13] The Senoi culture is not the only traditional society to provide children with instructions about dreaming. The anthropological literature contains other references to parents offering dream guidance to children as young as two.[14]

In comparison with the Senoi, we live in a highly heterogeneous society, characterized by spiritual, social, and political diversity. Nevertheless, the Senoi approach supplies a glimpse of the potential of dream education for children, and it has inspired new perspectives for guiding children in the art of dreaming. We have learned from the Senoi that we can help children grow in their ability to dream. We have learned that bad dreams may be redemptive and serve a child's growth. And we have learned that there is value in cultivating a relationship with the dream world early on.

Contrast this discovery of a traditional society's
approach to dreams with historical dream research in the
West. Here, the work with children's dreams began in the
early 1900s with the first child psychoanalysts. Sigmund
Freud devoted only a small proportion of his work to
young people's dreams. "The dreams of little children are
simple fulfillment of wishes," he wrote, "and as compared, therefore, with the dreams of adults, are not at all
interesting."[15] Later on, Freud acknowledged a particularly elaborate and rich quality in the dreams of four- and
five-year-olds. Though recognizing their fascinating content, Freud nevertheless ignored the possibility that childhood dreams might play an important role in children's
development.

Freud's theory of the unconscious and of repressed
infantile sexuality, however, laid the groundwork for the
first child psychoanalysts, among them Susan Isaacs,
Anna Freud, and Melanie Klein. Melanie Klein emerged
as one of the most prominent child psychoanalysts. Since
the repression of childhood impulses and experiences is
at the heart of adult neurosis, reasoned Klein, if we could
analyze children early on, we could prevent the development of neurosis in the adult. Animated by this belief,
Melanie Klein analyzed the dreams of child patients and
eventually developed her analysis through play. She subjected the elements of a child's play to an analysis similar to the inquiry she used on the child's dreams. Klein
recommended that child analysts not hesitate to communicate to children the dream interpretations that could
alleviate their anxiety.[16] In other words, for the sake of
alleviating suffering in children, Klein encouraged what
may well have been false interpretations, thereby dis-

torting the influence of dreams on the young subjects'
maturation.

The first interpretations of children's dreams came
from a medical orientation that looked for psychological
illness. The dreams of children came to be perceived as
thwarted wishes. "We find in them," said Anna Freud,
"the complicated distortions of wish fulfillment that correspond to the complicated neurotic organization of the
child patient."[17] Too often through the psychoanalytical
interpretation of children's dreams, both the child and the
dream were lost in the service of a theory initially conceived for neurotic adults, and later adapted for children.

The Swiss psychiatrist Carl Jung reacted to Freud's
theory of repressed infantile sexuality as too reductive.
Jung thought that explaining a child's psychology only
with reference to sexual energy overlooked the many
other types of energy that occur in a child's experience.
Jung, who himself had powerful dreams as a child, recognized the significance of childhood dreams. "Terrifying
or encouraging," commented Jung, "these farseeing
dreams and images appear before the soul of the child,
shaping his whole destiny."[18] Jung showed that beyond
the personal unconscious where memories of childhood
are stored is the collective unconscious from which universal dream motifs arise. His evidence for the collective
unconscious led Jung to say that the child's psyche was of
infinite extent and of incalculable age.[19]

Jung's dynamic theory of the psyche and his conception of the unconscious set the stage for a new
approach to the dreams of children. The most famous
child analyst to be inspired by Jung's work was the
American psychologist Frances Wickes. In her beautiful

book *The Inner World of Childhood,* Wickes, in contrast to Melanie Klein, warned against the danger of prematurely interpreting a child's dream, and in so doing injuring the "mysterious process" of the dream and the potential for transformation that the dream contains. Wickes advocated treating a child's dream "reverently" as a gift the child has given us.[20]

Whereas Freud and Jung approached the child's dream from a clinical perspective, the Swiss scientist Jean Piaget studied the role that dreams play in a child's cognitive development. Piaget criticized Freud's theory that the function of dreams is to disguise. On the contrary, thought Piaget, a dream is an attempt at consciousness, a way of knowing. Piaget showed that, through dreaming and playing, children assimilate their world—*take it in*—and that playing and dreaming are in the service of a child's development.[21] Piaget's work revolutionized our understanding of a child's mental development. Piaget helped us recognize that a child's magical thinking is a meaningful stage in a child's cognitive development and that symbolic thinking, as in dreams and play, is a genuine form of thought.

As our understanding of child psychology progressed over the century, child psychoanalysts grew more prudent in their interpretations of children's dreams. Many of them came to see dreams as a resource for a child's imagination in the service of that child's development. Child analysts Steven Luria Ablon and John E. Mack believed that children's dreams describe, in imaged form, the most pressing tasks and dilemmas children face at different stages of their development.[22] Child analysts also developed more creative approaches to working with children's dreams. Rudolph Ekstein compared a child's dream to a fairy tale that describes a conflict and, at the same time, contains a method of adaptation.[23] Others, like child psychiatrist Maurice R. Green, conceived of children's dreams as a resource for their imagination worth developing for its own sake.[24] Evidently, these professionals were at last arriving at conclusions that approached Senoi philosophy, but the act of teaching about and nurturing dreams was still only therapeutic, well outside the bounds of the family.

Since the beginning of the twentieth century, when Freud first saw dreams as the royal road to the unconscious and began using them in psychoanalysis, dreams had been the prerogative of clinicians. Over time, however, the interest in dreams grew beyond clinical circles. In the sixties, dreamwork with groups gained in popularity. Dream classes were offered in colleges, churches, and psychological societies. Dreamwork was made accessible to everyone through the publication of a large number of books on dreams.

Soon the way was open for dream education. Child therapist Richard M. Jones turned to teachers to use children's dreams for educational purposes. Jones contrasted dream interpretation with dream enjoyment. If, in adulthood, each has its place, observed Jones, for children, dream enjoyment is all. "The thing not to do with children's reported dreams," he suggested, "is to interpret them. The thing *to do* is more difficult: enjoy them, entertain them, draw them out, relate to them, embellish them, and, sometimes, put them to work in the service of developing not insights, but outsights."[25]

Elena Goldstein Werlin used dreams in her classroom to develop children's creativity and imagination.[26] The poet Kenneth Koch taught children to write poetry using their dreams.[27] In Caroline DeClerque's dream workshop, she asked children to dance their dreams, to render them through music, painting, drawing, or sculpture, and to look for alternatives to the ending of their dreams.[28] Other initiatives inspired by the Senoi aimed at teaching school-children to cultivate an active and confrontive attitude in their dreams.[29]

From the clinic to the classroom, we approached a new threshold: parenting with dreams. Patricia Garfield's *Your Child's Dreams* presented the Senoi approach to a readership of parents.[30] In *Dreamcatching,* Alan Siegel and Kelly Bulkeley encouraged the sharing of dreams within families; they focused on nightmares and their remedies and made room for children's spiritual dreams.[31]

Dreamguider: Open the Door to Your Child's Dreams explores ways of guiding children in Western families in the art of dreaming. It takes the reader to the heart-filled experience of sharing a young child's dreams day to day through dream journaling. And by laying the foundation for learning how to guide a beginning dreamer through dream challenges, it teaches *dreamguiding.*

Dreamguider draws from my long engagement in the study and research of children's dreams, from my experience in child development, and from my experience as a parent. Though addressed to adults, my book is ultimately an invitation to children and future generations to find, as my family and the families I've worked with have found, a path that weaves dreamtime into awake time and awake time into dreamtime, that we might create a legacy of closer, healthier families and communities.

Chapter One

Born from the Dream

The Dream of the Unborn Child

Your child's dream life has its roots in the womb. Every infant born appears to be emerging as if from the dream, when one weighs evidence from scientists who have penetrated the realm of sleep during the last sixty years. How did they find out that behind the little closed orbs, rimmed with a fringe of newborn lashes, a dream-like state was already pulsating?

Scientists began by challenging the common assumption that sleep was uniform throughout the night. When you put your toddler down for the night, you might think that his or her slumber will be all one thing till morning, but in fact it is not. Sleep researchers H. Davis and P. A. Loomis were the first to demonstrate, in 1937, that sleep occurs in four stages, progressing from the lightest to the deepest sleep, and then in a reversed way proceeds back to the lightest sleep again. Four or five times a night, your sleeping child goes through such a sleep cycle. Each cycle lasts on average ninety to 110 minutes, but the ratio between lighter and deeper sleep changes from one cycle to the next. The deeper sleep decreases as the night progresses, while the lighter sleep increases.[1] The last phase of light sleep in the morning can be as long as twenty minutes. The dreams your child awakens with in the morning occur during this last phase of light sleep.

The discovery of "rapid eye movement" during sleep (REM sleep) more than a decade later revolutionized the study of dreaming. And children's sleep was part of that discovery. In the fifties, Eugene Aserinsky observed that infants moved their eyeballs while they slept. Did adults also move their eyeballs as they slept, and if so, how did eye movement correlate with the stages of sleep? By measuring the electrical activity of the brains of adults while they slept, Aserinsky and Nathaniel Kleitman tracked their sleep cycles. Simultaneously, they recorded their eye movement. The two researchers discovered that rapid eye movement occurs at the end of a sleep cycle, when sleep is the lightest.[2,3] From then on, this light phase of sleep, characterized by rapid eye movement at the end of a sleep cycle, came to be known as REM sleep.[4] Soon after, William Dement and Nathaniel Kleitman began researching REM sleep and they confirmed the relationship between rapid eye movement and dreaming.[5] Dreams predominated during REM sleep. For the first time, dreams could be studied in sleep laboratories. Research on REM sleep and dreams boomed after that in the sixties and seventies. Some of this research focused on children, with the startling discovery that the younger the child, the more REM occurred!

The ratio of REM to total sleep time is at its highest before birth. While still in the warmth of the womb, your unborn child experiences the highest ratio of REM to total sleep time that he or she will ever experience for the rest of his or her entire life. Think of what this means: the stage of sleep associated with the most dreaming activity characterizes the pre-birth infant.

Scientists inferred that children experience REM sleep from before birth from evidence of REM sleep in preemies. An infant born prematurely at thirty weeks, for instance, spends 80 percent of his or her total sleep in REM sleep.[6] This ratio tapers off gradually toward birth and through infancy to stabilize at age three. In the newborn, it drops to 60 percent. Between three and a half and five months, it falls to 40 percent, and again at age one to 30 percent. By age three, children spend 20 percent of their total sleep in REM sleep, which is the same proportion of REM sleep as in adults.[7]

The high proportion of REM sleep from the very beginning of life raises the question of when a child's dream life begins. If children experience REM sleep from before birth, what is the function of REM sleep in the unborn child, in the newborn, and in the infant, if not to dream? And if so, what is the dream of the unborn child, of the newborn, and of the infant? Some researchers speculated that before visual perception and visual memory are acquired, dreaming might take olfactory, gustatory, tactile, or kinesthetic forms.[8] Others suggested that REM sleep in the young child serves to take in information received from the external world and to consolidate the developing structures for perception and memory. The fact that these structures are relatively undeveloped at birth could account for the high proportion of REM sleep in the newborn and in the first months of life.[9]

How is REM sleep in the unborn child related to the appearance of dreaming later on? We do not know. It is very likely, however, that the two are related developmentally and that the appearance of dreaming arises from early REM sleep beginning in the secret of the womb.

REM sleep correlates with the evolutionary development of the brain and it is also found in animals. Cats spend 20 to 60 percent of their total sleep in REM sleep, monkeys 11 to 25 percent, rats 15 to 20 percent, and sheep 2 to 3 percent. Birds, whose brains are little developed, spend only 1 percent of their total sleep in REM sleep. Does this mean that birds, rats, cats, sheep, and monkeys dream? When they are in REM sleep, animals gesture and mimic facial expression. But do they see images? "It is often assumed that all mammals dream," observed Jean Piaget, "but a dog which growls in its sleep is not necessarily evoking mental images and its 'dream' can be interpreted in terms of mere sensory-motor automatisms. Chimpanzees, too, dream, and in their case it is possible that there are images since they have a rudimentary symbolic function power."[10]

At what point dreaming begins in the evolutionary chain of species, within each species, and in the infant, remains open to speculation. Given the frequency of REM in preemies, it seems likely that the unborn child spends most of its sleep time in REM sleep, which is the ground for dreaming in adults. This circumstance calls our attention to the significance of REM sleep before birth and in the early stages of life, and to the role it may play in the

development of the dreaming mind and in the development of the whole child.

When pregnant, honor the moment and attune with
the dream pulse of your unborn one.

Dream Smiles of the Infant

Some researchers maintain that dreaming can be
traced back at least to the first year of life. Before a child
begins to speak, they can only infer dreaming by the child's
behavior during sleep. Hermine von Hug-Hellmuth, in
1919, cited the case of a child younger than one year old
who, having spent a day in the country playing at splashing water, reproduced similar splashing motions in his
sleep at night.[11] Milton H. Erickson observed activity in a
sleeping eight-month-old girl that resembled the play she
had enjoyed with her father before the evening meal.[12]
When you watch and listen to your own sleeping infant,
you might find examples of such meaningful behavior.

In contrast to adults, in whom there is a general
reduction of the muscular tonus during REM sleep, in
children, there is a noticeably higher frequency of movements: fluttering of the eyelids, rapid movements of the
eyeballs, larger movements of the limbs, vocalizations,
and irregular breathing. These movements in children
begin sometimes ten minutes before the onset of REM
sleep, then diminish toward the end of it. Observing your
child asleep, you've doubtless seen this for yourself. This
is why REM sleep in young children is sometimes called
"agitated" or "active sleep." Very intense in the first weeks,
children's bodily movements during REM sleep continue
until adolescence.[13]

Sleep laboratory observations of children's active sleep add a new dimension to the clinical observations of von Hug-Hellmuth and Erickson. Whereas these early researchers inferred dreaming from what they saw as meaningful gesturing during an infant's sleep, modern laboratory research added another layer. It confirmed that "active sleep" in children of all ages coincides with REM sleep, itself associated with dreaming. When your infant smiles in his or her sleep, vocalizes or gestures, you might infer that he or she is in REM sleep. You might also surmise that your child is having a dream.

At First, the One-Image Dream

Once your toddler begins to speak, the guesswork is over. Listeners know that children dream. A child might speak in his or her sleep or wake up telling of what he or she saw in a dream. I am characterizing children's first dreams as "one-image dreams" because young children describe them in a single phrase.

The literature on dreams provides examples of verbal manifestations of dreaming in children younger than two years old. Susan Isaacs reported the case of a fourteen-month-old, who had awakened frightened, saying that a white rabbit was about to bite him.[14] Selma H. Fraiberg tells of a fifteen-month-old boy who during his sleep yelled, "Let me down, let me down." He had been tied to the examination table at the doctor's that day.[15] John E. Mack refers to the nightmare of a thirteen-month-old during which he yelled, "Boom boom," which was what he usually yelled at the sight of a vacuum cleaner.[16]

Intent on characterizing the appearance of symbolic thinking in children as manifested in play and dreams, Jean Piaget observed the first signs of dreaming in children between the ages of twenty-one months and two years. Again, the children spoke in their sleep or woke yelling from a dream. "Poupette is back," screamed a two-year-old (2:2)* as she woke up, Piaget reported. She had met Poupette the day before and Poupette had used her toys too liberally.[17]

From a parent's standpoint, it usually seems that the predominant emotion that accompanies these early dreams is *fear*—fear of an animal, fear of a machine, fear of a peer invading one's territory, and in the case of the boy who had been tied to the examination table, terror, anger, and revolt. Screaming and sobbing, the child sometimes asks for help. "Pider on Sophia . . . off Sophia's leg . . . Dad, no more pider please!" pleads two-year-old Sophia (2:1) to her dad, Alan Siegel, who recounts Sophia's nightmare in *Dreamcatching*. As her dad comforts her, Sophia continues to sob, saying, "Sophia scared."[18]

A child's fear in dreams is an invitation to growth. This topic is at the core of chapters 6 and 7.

---

*To identify the age of the children whose dreams are described, I use numbers in parentheses: the first is how many years old the child is, the second adds the months to those years. For instance, the two-year-old who dreamed of Poupette was two years and two months old when she had the dream. Therefore "(2:2)" is used to designate her age.

A Beginning Dreamer:
Three- and Four-Year-Olds

Between ages three and five, children are likely to report their first dreams. The average dream can be compared to a narrative with introduction, development, crisis, and resolution. In the dreams of beginning dreamers, parents can recognize such narratives in rudimentary form. This points to a new benchmark in growth for the child.

At three, the dream reports are still very brief, so much so that they may leave you the listener yearning for more. One or two sentences are common: "Mamsie and Eddy were waving at me. Then we went to Disneyland. That's my dream" (3:2). "There was a witch who wanted to eat me. I said no!" (3:2). "There was a lizard on the chair who tried to eat me" (3:4). Soon longer dreams, three lines and more, appear, interspersed with the short dreams. Gradually, these longer dreams become the new norm and many of them show the complexity characteristic of dreams. "I dreamt of a baby. My baby was in a box inside the car. The box was glued to the car. I took the baby and I hugged him so tight and I loved him so much. The baby was Jack" (3:4). "There was a rattlesnake and I didn't run as fast as I could and he crawled up to here (my neck) and he was about to bite me" (3:8). "There was a dog and he came up to me. He was a big dog, and I wasn't even scared of him, even [though] I was only three and three-quarters and I played with him" (3:10).

Most three-year-olds' dreams portray situations and characters related to the child's daily life, although the previous examples show that witch and animal dreams appear early on. In contrast to what scientific literature would lead us to believe, the dreams of three-year-olds show a variety of feelings including fear, sadness, and love.[19] The witch and rattlesnake dreams also reveal that even young children show the potential for responding to the challenges that their dreams present. "I said no!" one three-year-old told the witch who wanted to eat her. "I didn't run as fast as I could," said another of his attempt to get away from the rattlesnake.

Dream reporting in young children is irregular. A three-year-old may report anywhere from zero to nine or so dreams in a month, occasionally including two dreams a day; the average is three dreams per month. By three years old, children begin to notice the difference between dream and reality. Nevertheless, three-year-olds, and older children as well, commonly blur the boundaries between dreams and waking fantasy. Dreams impact children's imaginations. Children may spontaneously act on their dreams, develop them into imaginary narratives, or amplify them through imaginary play. In chapter 3, you will learn about the value of children's spontaneous "dreamwork" through dream developments and how to integrate your child's dream developments when dream journaling together.[20]

As a child nears age four, with an ever-more-bold imagination, the child's dreams get longer and more articulate. And children begin to find their style as dream tellers. Dream reports flow with ease, lengthening to include sometimes ten to fifteen lines. Although a four-year-old may recall longer dreams, the frequency of dream reporting remains the same as it was at three.

Most dreams continue to portray the child's personal life: school situations, interactions with friends, family adventures. In addition, the dreams of a four-year-old include threatening animals and encounters with witches, monsters, dinosaurs, and giants. In these encounters, the child struggles to overcome the dream threat. A child takes his toy sword to fight a dream witch. Another throws "a dummy and forty clubs" at the threatening dinosaurs of her dream.

Children that age dwell in the realm of magic like fish in water. As mentioned, Piaget called the thinking of preschoolers "magical thinking." Young magical thinkers, Piaget observed, account for powerful phenomena with fantastic explanations. For instance, "the clouds move because God blows on them." "The moon follows me at night when I walk." "The waves are alive because they move. The curtains too are alive, because they too move." We adults marvel at the explanations our children concoct. Where do they come up with these ideas, we ask ourselves. Not surprisingly, magical elements appear in dreams at that stage: magical occurrences, objets, or animals endowed with magical powers, such as magical sticks, magical rings, or magical horses. Children's developing imagination is also exposed to stories, television, and games that feed their ingenuity, fantasies, and dreams.

Through the practice of dreaming and dream reporting, a child's dream awareness gradually awakens and develops. Four-year-olds can become conscious, for instance, that the dream ends when they open their eyes. They become increasingly aware that there is more to the dream than what they can report: "There's lots more, but I can't remember." Unexpectedly, a child might also express puzzlement at the nature of a dream. "How could you guys be in it, if you didn't even have that dream?" reflected a four-year-old to his parents after telling a dream in which the parents appeared. Such remarks show how a child ponders a phenomenon as complex as dreams. When privileged to witness such spontaneous insights, savor the moment. Your child's questions are the seed of future knowledge.

A Child's Dream Life Blossoms: Five- and Six-Year-Olds

At five, a child's dream life blossoms. Dream reports double in length and children report twice as many dreams as they did at three and at four. Age five brings significant dreams. As the child's world expands, the content of the dreams also diversifies to include a larger variety of themes and more remote settings: park, school, circus, travel. The dreams of five-year-olds are even richer in symbolic images: animals, kings and queens, forests, mountains, oceans, dragons, fairies, and monsters. Unknown boys, girls, and adults appear more frequently in the dreams. Five-year-olds may also begin to show a sense of privacy about their dreams.

Five-year-olds become capable of new levels of awareness within their dreams. Their ability to respond to dream challenges is enhanced. Their reports of their dreams may reflect their sensations and feelings in the dream as well as the choices they made in response to dream challenges. Further development in dream awareness becomes possible. In a flash of lucidity, a five-year-old suddenly grew

aware of dreaming while dreaming: "Then I noticed that
I was sleeping and that I was dreaming. I said to you and
Dad, 'I'm dreaming! I'm dreaming!'"

The first elements of flying may appear in the dreams
of five-year-olds, and sometimes before. Flying at this age
may occur as an extension of running or jumping. In the
dreams of young children, flying is brief and often limited in height. Children may fly in a balloon, on a flying
carpet, in a plane. They may fly as birds, as bumblebees,
or as themselves, mirroring their emerging independence
and self-reliance.

Whereas younger children often alter a dream report,
by the time they are five years old, children are becoming
aware that they have done so and may mention it. Nevertheless, five-year-olds occasionally straighten up what is
illogical in a dream, fill in the gaps, or change details as
they tell and retell a dream.

After peaking at five, the frequency of dream reporting begins a downward curve as the child enters first
grade. A new humor often permeates the dreams of
adventure of six-year-olds. A sudden perception of death
may also come through the child's dreams. A six-year-old
is an established dreamer.

A child's dream awareness reaches new levels of
refinement, as in "I had another dream, a short dream
that led to this dream." Dream alteration is reduced to a
minimum, although a six-year-old can still turn a dream
into a tall tale and take pleasure in it, or spontaneously act
out a dream after telling it. Occasionally, the dream of a
five- or six-year-old shows signs of precognition.

Taking Flight:
Seven- and Eight-Year-Olds, and Older

As children enter the last stage of childhood, age seven to puberty, their relationship to the dream world changes. Young children blur the boundaries between dream and daytime fantasy, but by seven years old, the difference between the two becomes clear and irreversible. It is a matter of cognitive development and understanding what a dream is: "A dream is a night event. A fantasy is something that I make while I'm awake." At this age, children who report a dream limit themselves to the dream report and unequivocally demonstrate awareness of the dream experience as separate and distinct. Here the gaps are identified and not filled. And although the older child may still engage in fantasy following the report of a dream, the children I studied were quick to say, "But don't write this down. It is not part of the dream."

Children at this age begin to have some perspective on their dream life as a whole: "I often fly in my dreams, I love those dreams," or "I have had that dream over and over again." The child begins to wonder about the meaning of dreams: "I am often chased in my dreams. I wonder what it means." Or the child exclaims, "I know why I had that dream!" The child is old enough to recognize real life events that might be associated with the dream and may make the connections. As they continue to grow, children ten and older spontaneously try to make sense of their dreams.

Whereas the younger child is ready to step back into the dream and enact it live, the older child emerges from the dream and reflects on it. As school continues to dominate the child's life, the frequency in dream reporting further drops to the level when the child first began reporting dreams at three and four. On the other hand, the child is capable of accessing new depths of the dream world: "I had a dream in my dream." As the tone in dream telling becomes more temperate, the richness in dream imagery remains undiminished.

Although the first elements of flying in dreams may appear at earlier stages, the ability to fly in dreams really blossoms during this last stage of childhood.[21] Flying may occur as a result of falling from a height in a dream; for instance, falling out of an airplane or being pushed off a building by a very strong wind. At other times, the dreamer takes off directly from the ground. Flying can also be induced by means of a magic device: Peter Pan's fairy dust, a flying cape, a magical pot. The flight might be directed vertically and upward or horizontally, as in long-distance flying. A friendly adult—a parent, a caretaker, a friend—sometimes accompanies the dreamer on a flying adventure. Flying in a dream remains occasional and a moment of grace. Flying in dreams awaits further developments in speed, distance, height, and control—all expressive of the child's increasing capabilities in later stages of dreaming development.

From the earliest age, in their dreams, your children receive challenges that they are called to encounter with courage, bravery, humor, love, and burgeoning wisdom.

Once a child begins to speak, we can witness and appreciate the child's dream life with more assurance. A child's dream awareness gradually develops until the dream stands on its own as a separate and distinct occurrence at the end of early childhood. At any age along the way, your child's dreams are a window into his or her many-splendored heart and mind.

Because children are fresh to life and unfettered by practicality and responsibilities, they naturally come closest to embracing our primal legacy to practice the art of dreaming. Who better to teach parents and all adults the refinements of dreamguiding?

Chapter Two

What Children Believe
about Dreams

Already dreaming in Technicolor night after night, yet having no knowledge of psychology, children develop their own beliefs about dreams. Fresh in their explanations, young children may believe that dreams come from the moon, that they dream with their eyes open, or that dreams are made of rainbows.

Until age six or seven, a young child's concept of the dream is still in formation. Listening to your child's dreams, you may, as if from the corner of your eye, catch a glimpse of your child's early beliefs about dreams. You may also appreciate the process by which girls and boys sort out a phenomenon as complex as dreaming. For instance, your son may insist that the scratches on his bedroom door were left by the wolves that came in the night. Or your daughter might seem to mingle dream and thought as if they were one, as Marie (3:2) does in the following example. "This morning I was thinking of a pink dress and a pink shirt and I danced in it. Will you buy it for me?" asked Marie, as she walked into her dad's office, just after waking up one early morning. Evidently, for a young child, the difference between a dream and a thought is imprecise, since both seem to have happened to them.

Dreaming and dream reporting provide your child firsthand experience to figure out this reality. Note that the child's ability to dream and to report dreams does not depend on having a fully formed concept of dreams. As shown in chapter 1, children can and do report dreams early.

Researchers have laid the groundwork for under-standing how a child's conception of dreams develops. Jean Piaget, who revolutionized our views on children's cognitive development, was the first, in 1926.[1] Whereas an adult takes for granted that a dream is an inner, immaterial, and individual experience, Piaget said, a child grows into knowing that. Since then, other researchers have enriched the topic. My own interviews with children on their views on dreams were illustrative, and I share some of them here.

Where Do Dreams Come From?

Young children have dreams whose contents are outside the boundaries of their waking consciousness, so they usually do not hesitate to accept that dreams come from an external source rather than from within them. Dreams come "through the window from the other side of the forest," one child says. They come from "the night," they come from "the moon," others contend. Dreams come from "the tooth fairy," or they come "from foreign countries," still others assert. Or, like Mariya, they believe that they are delivered from afar.

Mariya (4:11) draws herself in her mom's bed with a high arched headboard. "That's me," she says, "I am wearing lipstick. That's my pajama." Above her is the picture of her dream. "That's the dream I had and the park. That's the picnic blanket. Mommy gave me this picnic blanket," she adds. Then she moves on with the dream, "That's Lea. She's running away. That's her pants. You see her?" she asks. "That's the man who is running after her." At the level of Mariya's head and in the space next to the bed, we see a small opening, "That's the place where dreams come from," she says with resolve, as if dreams came from the other side through an opening in the fabric of the universe.

Having no proof to the contrary, children often believe that dreams are delivered from the foreign and faraway, and from the beings that dwell there. To children such explanations are more "logical" than adult theories, such as the "subconscious" and the "unconscious."[2] The explanations seem plausible because they can be pictured. Your own child probably has magnificent explanations of his or her own.

Natalie (3:6) points behind her head to show where dreams come from. They come "in the ear," says Al (4:6). Whereas these children attune to dreams as entering them from the outside, others experience the dreams as coming from inside, from the "mouth," from the "body."

Children come to realize, as they grow, that dreams are not delivered from afar, but instead arise from within their *head, mind, or imagination:* Dreams come "from the brain," says Brian (5:5). "I think they just come in your brain that way, and that way you would have a dream. . . . They just come." The more he thinks about it the firmer he gets: Dreams arise within the dreamer's brain. This viewpoint emerges as children develop, as they more frequently weigh their beliefs against their experience, against those of their peers, and against those of adults.

What is significant in the child's growing awareness of the head-mind-brain-imagination connection with the making of dreams is that it brings the child closer to the notion of dreams as an inner, individual, and immaterial experience. It does not differentiate between the faculties involved in the dreaming process. We can certainly not expect a child to differentiate between the brain, the mind, and the imagination and the role that they play in the dreaming process. We would be at a loss to spell this out ourselves. We must also acknowledge that dreams take us beyond the mind as well.

The heart of Piaget's theory, which grew by the mid-twentieth century to wide acceptance, is that a child's cognitive development occurs as a result of direct experience. Piaget showed that cognitive development occurs in stages, and he posited that those stages were the same in every culture. Other theoreticians of the same era emphasized the role of culture and environment. A child's understanding of dreams comes as a result of interplay between culture and development.

Children elaborate points of view to explain the occurrence of dreams. How do they justify the formation of dream images in their dream mind? "When there's a dog," explains Mariya, "he puts it on my head, then there's a bone. When a paper comes . . . you get the paper." In other words, if a dog comes and puts a bone on the sleeping child's head, the child dreams of a bone. If a paper comes, the child dreams of a paper. The dream image is created by whatever happens to come into physical contact with the sleeper's head. For Lucie (5:10), the dream image is not created from direct contact with an object, but from the projection of pictures onto the dreamer's mind. "In our head," explains Lucie, "it is a photograph that shows, and it thinks in our head. It's someone else, in his home. He has a big piece of cardboard. And pictures pass on it. He shows and it makes in our head." Like a screen, the dream mind that Lucie describes receives pictures that someone else sends to the dreamer from a distance.

As their minds develop, children rework these points of view in ever more comprehensive and adapted models, always motivated by the desire to make sense of their world. Most parents in our culture help their children understand the difference between dreams and waking reality, so that what children believe approaches the adult viewpoint. By contrast, too seldom do parents reinforce the connection between dreams and waking reality. This connection is the opportunity that dreamguiding reinforces. Dreamguiding teaches parents that dreams are not disconnected from waking reality, but are manifestations designed to help that reality occur more smoothly. In fact, as you will soon recognize, the difference between dreams and waking reality is far less important than their dynamic relationship.

What Do Children Believe
Dreams Are Made Of?

For children, who still accept dreams as substantive, dreams have irrefutable physicality, like Peter Pan's shadow in Sir James M. Barrie's novel. As the story of *Peter Pan* begins, Peter Pan returns to the Darling household to retrieve his shadow, which he finds in a chest of drawers. Wendy then sews the shadow back onto him. Peter Pan's shadow is tangible. Is a dream, to a child, tangible like the shadow of Peter Pan? When asked if anyone could see her dream inside her head while she was dreaming, Rosie (3:10) spontaneously said no. When asked why, she answered candidly, "Because it's stuck . . . on my neck."

What are dreams made of for a young child? "Dreams are made of metal," says Peter (5:8). "Because I once dreamt that there was a guy who had shot a bullet, and the bullet had gotten all smashed on me. And it had fallen on the ground." Dreams are made of "sugar," some children say. Others believe they are made of paper, of threads, of iron, of wood. Materials children say dreams are made of include solid and airy materials alike. Dreams are made "of rainbow," believes Helen (3:8). They are made of "voice," says Rosie (3:10). Dreams are made of "glue," states Richard (4:2). They are made of "clouds, of rainbow and butterflies," asserts Mariya (4:11).

If children believe that dreams are tangible, do they also believe that they can touch their dreams? Some young children say no, not because dreams are intangible, but "because it's way up" (3:8), "because you're sleeping" (3:10), "because you don't know where it is" (4:3).

Some say yes, you can touch your dream. "I can touch it," says Mariya, as she points to her tummy.

The older they get, the more reflective children become. "I think when you touch them, you don't have your dream, says Lisa (5:0). "If I go touch them," speculates Peter (5:8), "I will do sleepwalking, I say, because they're further away than me . . . about on my bedroom door." "If I touch them like this," gestures Françoise (5:9), as if touching a light balloon floating in midair, "it will go somewhere else." For Charles, an older five-year-old, dreams are made "of images," and one can touch them, but they are very thin. "It is very thin. It is thinner than that. "Look," demonstrates Charles, bringing the palms of his hands together. "You see my hands? You have to stick them together. It's that thin."

Gradually, children grow to understanding that dreams are made of *pictures, thoughts,* and *imagination* and that one cannot touch them. "It's made with memory," says Katherine (5:11), "like me—I have good memory." Can one touch dreams? No, believes Katherine, unless one dreamt of touching them. Otherwise dreams are untouchable.

What Part of the Child's Body Dreams?

Children know that the dreams happened because they experience dreaming with different parts of their bodies: tummy, heart, mouth, eyes. "Um," says Terra (4:4), considering thoughtfully what part of her body she dreams with, "with my tummy." "With my mouth," says Rosie (3:10), in answer to the same question. I dream with "my heart," asserts Mariya forcefully. "That's where my heart is," she adds, lifting her dress and pointing to her tummy.[3] At five, Julie specifies that she dreams "with my whole body, with my arms and all." (Julie may have been referring to her "dream body" here rather than to the organ with which she understands herself to dream.) Alan (4:9) and Annie (6:3) assert, as other children often do, that they dream with their "eyes," because they "see" when they dream. Other children might say that the dream is "in their eyes."[4]

Children also naturally point to, or name, their forehead as the organ they dream with. "I had a dream in here," says young Marie (3:6), pointing to her forehead." Audrey (4:10) shares a similar view. So does Todd (5:0) and he explains why, "'Cause the forehead thinks what kind of dream you get to have . . . and then the dream comes."[5] The older they get, the more likely children are to say, as Oliver (4:9) did, that they dream "with my head," or as Todd (5:5) did, "with your brain."

A child grows to understand that the *mind-imagination-head* somehow manufactures dreams, yet this is but the first step in acknowledgment of the child's participation in the making of his or her dreams.

Where Is the Dream Located?

The process of identifying where the dream originates, as well as which senses experience it, is hand in glove with figuring out where the dream is. Is the dream in the bedroom? Does the child leave the bed to find the dream? Or does the dream deliver other places to the child dreamer's mind?

For the young child, the dream has a location; for

instance, in the bedroom, on the window, on the door, the wall, near the child, on the pillow. For Mara (5:4), "It's in Mom's bedroom." When asked whether their dream is inside or outside, many young children, like Mara, believe that it is "outside." Other children see it both ways. Joanna (4:5) reasons that the dream goes in and out of the brain and thus is both inside and outside. "I see it inside of me," says Joanna, "but it's really outside . . . Well, it pops out and it's really invisible. And it pops out and I can see it and then it goes back inside of me and then I can't see it anymore. That's what happens to me sometimes." Todd (5:5) shares a similar view: "It comes outside your brain and back inside."

Children often report dreams that take place in their bedroom. "I was in bed," says Peter (5:8). "I saw a small animal. The animal stuck its tongue out and I saw that it was a snake." The child finds a bedroom full of possibility and refuge, full of enjoyment and deliverance, and has an unusually large amount of attention for events and supposed events in that bedroom.

Not only do young children commonly believe that their dream is "in the bedroom," but they also believe that they dream with their eyes wide open. When a child believes that he or she dreams with wide-open eyes, it takes only one more step for this child to conclude that any outside observer might also see his or her dream. Here is a conversation with Mariya:

> When you have a dream and you are sleeping—let's pretend your mommy comes into room while you are dreaming—could she see your dream?
> No.

Why?
'Cause I close my eyes. I mean I don't close my eyes. I think I will have a nightmare again. I don't like nightmares.

No, no one likes nightmares. So, do you dream with your eyes closed or your eyes open?
Open.

You dream with your eyes open. If your mom comes into your room while you are dreaming, can she see your dream?
[If] she came and she would get my Beanie Baby.

She would get your Beanie Baby.
Then she'd see my dream.

When children are in transition between two stages of development, they typically struggle with contradictory points of view. Stephan just turned six. For him, dreams come "from me," "from my head." But he also believes that he dreams sometimes with his eyes closed and sometimes with his eyes open and that the dream is accordingly sometimes inside and sometimes outside. Here is our exchange on the subject:

When you dream, where is your dream?
I don't know.

Does the dream take place in you or in your room?
In my room.

When you dream, are your eyes closed or open?
Sometimes they're open. Sometimes they're closed.

When your eyes are closed, where is your dream?
Here. In my bedroom.

When your eyes are open, the dream is where, in you or in your room?
Ah, it's not what I meant. I meant the first thing that you said. It's because it's in the body. And the other thing that the eyes are open, I mean that it's in my room.

When your eyes are closed, it is inside your body, and when your eyes are open, it is in your room?
Yes, because I see it.

Where is it in your room?
Well, sometimes in my closet, [sometimes] in my parents' bedroom, over there.

If your mommy came into your room while you were dreaming, could she see your dream?
No.

Why can't she see your dream?
Because it's in my head.

Stephan tries to account for several contradictory points of view. The dream takes place outside (in the closet, in the parents' bedroom) and inside the body. And at the same time, no one else can see it because it is in the head. To accommodate these contradictory points of view, he will soon integrate them into a more differentiated and flexible concept of dreaming.

As long as a child believes that someone else can see a dream inside his or her head, the dream retains some measure of materiality. Five-year-old Todd understands that a dream is invisible to an outside observer. Yet he believes that if someone were to open his head while he was dreaming, this outside observer could see his dream:

> *When you dream, where is the dream?*
> I don't know.
>
> *Is it inside of you or outside of you?*
> I feel it is inside.
>
> *Where inside? [He points to his forehead.]*
> *There, in your forehead? [He nods.] If your mommy came into your room when you were dreaming, could she see your dream?*
> No.
>
> *Why?*
> Because, you see, when I see my mom asleep, I can't see what she's dreaming.
>
> *Yes, you're right. So that would be the same.*
> *If someone could open your head while you are dreaming—no one will do this, but let's pretend that someone could—could they see your dream inside your head?*
> I think they could.

Soon enough, children's magical beliefs melt away.
By age six and a half, children usually understand the
internal and immaterial character of dreams.[6] Children
then accept that dreams occur in the dreamer's mind,
head, or memory; that they dream with their eyes
closed; and that dreams are invisible, even inside the
head. So it is for Katherine (5:11) who is just about to
turn six:

> *When you dream, where is your dream?*
> It is in my head. But we always think that it's true
> when we sleep. Me, that's always what I do.

> *Is the dream in you or in your room?*
> In me.

> *When you dream is there something in front of you?*
> In front of me? Well, yes, in the dream. It is possi-
> ble if I dream of that. If I dream that my dream is in
> front of me. Sometimes I dream of that.

> *If your mommy came into your room when you were
> dreaming, could she see your dream?*
> No.

> *Why?*
> Because it would be in my memory anyway.

> *If I were in your room when you were having a dream,
> could I see your dream?*
> No. Just like my mom, 'cause it would be in my
> memory anyway.

If someone could open your head and look into it when you are having a dream, could they see your dream?

No. Because it's just something that I think all by myself. We cannot even see it in the head.

What an adult knows as a certainty, a child grows to realize. "I put two nails in my two fingers," dreams Marie (now 3:8), "and I pulled them out and put them in a box, but it was just a dream. I don't really have nails in my fingers." That the dream is "only a dream" means for Marie that she has distinguished the dreamworld from her waking world, not that she devalues dreaming. The realization that a dream is "only a dream," different from waking reality, can free the way for a child to begin understanding the dreamworld for its own sake and grow gradually more conscious within the dream state itself. This is only true, however, if the child, reinforced by those he or she respects (the *dreamguiders*), embraces the opportunity to honor the dream.

Children mature in their understanding of dreams whether their parents tell them anything or not. They are trying to figure out the world in which they live and their experience of it. Arriving at answers on the nature of dreams is no easy task even for us adults. So it is a monumental task when children grapple with such questions as: Where do dreams come from? What they are made of? What part of the body dreams? Where is the dream located? We can therefore be grateful for whatever they disclose about their inquiry.

It may only be when a child drops an unexpected remark that parents glimpse the child's early beliefs about dreams. These beliefs do not last. Soon they vanish and with them some of the charm of early childhood. But at every point along the way, a child's understanding of dreams reflects an intelligent act and a genuine form of thought that is developmentally consistent from generation to generation, not just among the Senoi, not just in the West, but everywhere.

This book's premise is that this intelligence and this genuine thought process are not just consistent, but necessary. As a parent and dreamguider, you need do nothing more than witness and celebrate your child's evolving beliefs. Take time to appreciate remarks that reflect your child's gradual grasp of a reality as complex as that of dreams. You will find that it is a very gratifying journey, for both of you.

Chapter Three

A Child's First Dream Journal

All dreams are ephemeral. Most fade in the morning light, then vanish irretrievably as one fully awakens. Even the most memorable, those we say we will never forget, lose their features as time passes. In children, for whom every day has much that is new, dreams tumble in and out of memory like so many breaths. This evanescence can intensify a parent's urge to chronicle a child's priceless treasures as they arrive. By keeping a dream journal, you and your child can collect dreams when they emerge and revisit them later.

By making a dream journal, parents can also watch and enjoy their children change and grow in a whole new way: through their dreams.

A Dream-Receptive Household

Experience teaches that creating an environment receptive to dreams beckons to dreams to show themselves more readily. The first step is to make dreams part of your household. Rarely in the West do dreams interest everyone in a family, yet all that is required is one parent or one sibling fascinated enough by his or her own dreams to talk about them. That one person gives sleeptime adventures a *presence,* an identity within the family. Appreciation for the world of dreams can induce a warm and familiar receptivity to a young child's dreams, a recognition that talking about a dream when it happens is allowed and even encouraged.

Sooner or later, there will be a "first" declared dream. Like the first tooth, the first step, the first word, a child's first dream comes unexpectedly. If your young child has not begun dreaming yet, do not press him or her for dreams. Somewhere between your child's third and fifth year, and sometimes earlier, the moment arrives. Your preschooler announces a dream. This may come without warning and even, if it is a nightmare, be unwanted. Your son or daughter may not know that it was a dream that occurred. Young children have few ways of separating dream events from daytime events. But happen it has, and he or she is telling you about it.

When a dream knocks at the door of your child's consciousness for the first time, welcome it. This is your opportunity to open the door to a child's world of dreams and to embrace the *dreamguider* within you, in earnest.

Dream Tellers

Before anything else, young children are *dream tellers.* As the parent, you are one of the first people your child will likely tell a dream to. A welcoming attitude toward your child's dreams encourages your budding dream teller. Your toddler's first dreams may only be sporadic, but soon your kindergartner and then your older child will delight you with ever-surprising dream adventures.

Your child's reminiscences about dreams can occur at any time: in the bathtub, in the car, or at night when your child is preparing for bed. Some of the very first images that children perceive come at the onset of sleep. Known as *hypnagogic images,* these are apt to be vivid. Even if benign, these images may scare the child because they are a new and unaccountable phenomenon. Mostly, however, like all of us, your child will remember and report dreams upon awakening.

Over time, you and your child will evolve your own ritual for dream telling. For instance, you might lie down on your child's bed every morning, as he or she spills the beans about nighttime experiences. You might "take dictation" while your child chats in the bath. Perhaps you sit down with your preschooler after the older children have left for school. Or your child shows up in your bedroom every morning with a dream and climbs into your bed for dream telling.

From one to three lines in the beginning, a child's dream reports gradually lengthen to three to ten lines, then to five to fifteen and up to rather intricate reports by age five. The word count of a child's first dreams around age three may be three to twelve words. Around age five, it can easily range between thirty-five and one hundred words, and sometimes more. Dream reports get rapidly longer, especially if given to an attentive listener.

With practice in dream telling, a child's narrative power gains in precision of detail. For instance, while a three-year-old might report that her dad was lying in a hammock, an eight-year-old might report that he lay in a hammock between two birch trees and was wearing a tie, a tie with golfers on it. An older child, nine-year-old Tiffany, who had been reporting her dreams from the time she was five, began a dream account with the following subtleties of details: "Me, you [dad], and Johnny were walking by Nathan's house. John was in the lead. Then Dad. Then me."

Although a dream is an involuntary occurrence, in contrast to a story, which involves more conscious participation, both are narratives. The average dream, like a story, includes a beginning, a culminating point, and a resolution. Note that as a dream teller, your young child is claiming and cultivating an important human ability: the *ability to tell a story.*

Significantly, my research illustrates a gulf between children who live with dream reporting and those who do not. For children who do not report their dreams for the first time until age eight, nine, ten, or even older, the reports are often as short as one to three lines, the length of reports from a three-year-old beginning dreamer. These young people are not used to people paying attention to their dreams, and they may not be accustomed to thinking reflectively about dreams.

With practice in dream telling, a child becomes skilled at mastering the difficult tasks of:

✳ *Paying attention to dreams*

✳ *Carrying dreams into waking consciousness*

✳ *Translating an image into words*

✳ *Reporting a dream verbally to another person*

The richness of the dream material itself nurtures a child's dream telling. The dream's images, its movement, emotional flavors, vivid colors, and the familiar and friendly characters it stages, as well as the new, surprising, and scary ones, combined with magical turns of events that delight, all make for good telling.

Your first task as a parent is to give attention. Attentive listening—receptive and without judgment, yet responsive—helps a child develop as a dream teller. As if clearing the land and hoeing in fertile soil, you prepare the attitudes, practices, and space for dreams that will last a lifetime. Remember that a dream is a creation of the unconscious, unintentional and unrepeatable. This might help you appreciate each dream that your child reports. A dream is not one in a million or one in a billion or a trillion. A dream is entirely unique in history. Try giving your full emotional presence to your little boy or girl who confides in you with the precious gift of his or her nighttime experience. It will spark your child's enthusiasm for dream telling. From this same emotional presence will spring your gratitude for your child's dream, your praise, and your occasional comment in response to your child's dream. (In chapter 7, you will find more on how to be responsive to your young child dreamer, guiding when called to do so.)

Children have their own individual styles as tellers of their dreams. Dream telling also varies with the dreams themselves. Some dreams are told matter-of-factly, whereas others take on epic proportions. The closer in time to the actual dream event the report comes, the truer to all of its details the telling will be, and the less likely that your child will have elaborated on it.

A child's dream account may begin with a usual phrase such as "I dreamed that . . ." Just as often, though, a child opens the dream by stepping directly into it with "I was in a little house" (5:9) or "It was all snowy and we were walking to the trains" (4:7). Age four to seven, they may begin with "Once upon a time" or one of its variations, such as "There once was . . ." or "One day . . ."

"We lived on the side of Georgia Montana," began seven-year-old Anna. "One day, on Easter, me and Harry were walking looking for elves. An old woman came past us. . . ." She went on, "We rushed back to the house, but before us flying with speed was Hunco, the Black Witch. (Some people call her the Devil.) She carried us with her magic into the head of the hill . . ." And so came forth Anna's encounter with the Black Witch. The "once upon a time" formula may indicate, although not necessarily, that the child has stepped into story time.

Dreams and the idea of dreams can stimulate the child's imagination. When you begin to wonder if your child is reporting a dream or dreaming live in front of your very eyes, it is best to delight in the wondrous adventures of your child's imagination without trying to figure out where dream telling ends and storytelling begins.

Children can charm you by using rhetorical questions to add drama to their dream telling:

> ✳ *And do you know who was in the race? [pause] The girl! (4:8)*

> ✳ *In the middle of our picnic came you-know-what? A triceratops. (5:11)*

> ✳ *I looked down and guess what it was? A diamond ring. I slipped it on my finger. And guess what it was? A magical ring. (4:10)*

Predictably, it is not uncommon for young children either to close the dream's delivery with the phrase "The End" or one of its variations such as "Bye" or "Amen," words they already associate with the termination of a story. These styled formulations show a sense that dreams, like stories, take the listener to another time dimension. Surely, they also show an aptitude for mimicry at a very young age. Impressively, the child has learned, from other family members, storytellers, television, books, and very likely from practice, just what it takes to keep an audience in thrall.

Recording a Child's Dreams

Capturing the dreams on paper serves several crucial purposes. Recording a dream as a child tells it communicates that you value both the dream and the telling. Also, it gives you both a growing archive of shared material.

Likely, your child will soon report a dream. That day, you may be, as I was with my daughter, moving quickly for the best way to "catch" the dream on the spur of the moment and in the most sensitive way. Shortly after my daughter turned three, she woke up one morning saying, "I had a dream." And she went on with the dream: "There was a snake that went on my wall." Even as a professional, I still felt unprepared for my own child's "big moment." I scrambled for my audiotape recorder, as I had done as a researcher. I did not want to miss anything she said. Nor did I want to appear distracted, so I turned the tape recorder on and focused on the dream, trying to be as unself-conscious as possible about the device.

"There was a snake that went on my wall and I was afraid," she said. "I killed it, then I ate it." She looked at me, as if to make sure I was fully understanding how important this was, then added, "That's the meaning of killing."

"How did you kill it?" I asked, trying to pull together more details.

"With a stick," she said forcefully.

I later transcribed the dream in the journal. It was the first that I wrote down. The point when children begin recounting their dreams is, in many ways, the beginning of a journey together. Your son or daughter is the leader, and you follow with curiosity, recording the details. Like a cartographer on an excursion, you begin the "paper trail."

My daughter, like most children, began to talk about her dreams when she was too little to write, so I recorded them in a small notebook. The other families I've worked with have done likewise. Becoming their child's scribe, they keep a traditional dream journal, assembling their children's dreams in chronological order and in one place.

The journal belongs close at hand, like any diary, and can be taken along on vacation, holding as it does a precious record of the unconscious. Dream recording can take place in many settings: in the child's bedroom, at the breakfast table, or in the tent in the mountains.

While dreaming, children experience vivid emotions. Sometimes a child awakens from a dream in tears, at other times afraid or in awe. When a child wakes up still fresh with the feeling of a dream, the first task is to follow the dream telling with your ears, eyes, and heart. The dream can always be recorded later from memory or from the child's dictation, once your child has led you through its terrain.

First dreams are short and easy to record. But soon, fed with attention by both parent and child, the dream reports lengthen and become elaborate. Sometimes the challenge of recording a dream from a child's dictation is to keep pace with the child's dream telling. At other times, the challenge is to stay with the thread of the dream, when the child strays and wanders to other topics.

Start by writing the date of the dream—day, month, and year. Children grow up quickly and the date of the dream will soon take on its full significance.

Recording the dream itself is fundamental. You will record it as your child reports it. But other pieces of information a child gives are worth recording, for the light they shed on a child's dream and what it means to the child. There is sometimes a preamble before your child launches into the dream proper. Regardless of the dream content, these remarks capture in a flash the feeling of a dream and reveal immediately how the dream sets with the child, as in the following examples, which could be from children of any age:

✸ *I had the most beautiful dream I ever had. I want this dream again and again.*

✸ *Oh, I had the saddest dream.*

✸ *I did not like the dream that I had.*

✸ *I had a scary dream.*

✸ *I had a nightmare.*

✸ *That was really a weird dream.*

✸ *This is the most fun dream I ever had.*

Other introductory remarks will tell you about your child's growing awareness within the dream state, as in:

✸ *After I closed my eyes and was in my bed, I saw the dream I had last night. (3:0)*

✸ *There's lots more, but I can't remember. (4:2)*

✸ *I had a dream I never had before. (5:7)*

✸ *I had another dream, a short dream that led to this dream. (6:9)*

✸ *I had a dream in my dream. (7:4)*

✸ *Recently when I have been dreaming, my dreams have been a lot longer the past few days. I don't know why. I'll wake up in the middle of the night. Then I go back to sleep and they last so long. I don't really remember. I just know they are a lot longer. (11:4)*

Next comes the dream. On some occasions, recording a child's dream is a leisurely experience, luxurious with time, including time for questions and time for drawing. On other days, it is hurried. Some dreams slip by unrecorded. Some, either because of their theme or the power of their images, we do not want to miss recording. Having heard only the gist of them, we look for the first opportunity to sit down with the child and record them. Over time, the dream journal builds up.

I suggest writing most dreams directly in the journal, as the child's report unfolds. Sometimes, however, it is easier to take the dictation on a separate sheet of paper, in order to write faster, albeit messier, without interrupting the flow with questions. Slowing down the child, in order to catch up with the writing, can also work. Record the dreams word for word from the child's dictation, if you can. If you cannot and have to paraphrase, be sure to reread your recorded version of the dreams aloud to your son or daughter, to check for accuracy. It is easy to introduce minor distortions. Give your child the opportunity to make corrections or add missing details.

Usually, the recording ends with the child's report. Occasionally, a child gives more than one version to a dream and can even embellish a dream into a make-believe narrative. Recording the changing details from one version to the next, and the imaginary narrative that might spring from a child's dream, tracks the process through which a child develops a dream. Enlarging on or refurbishing a dream actively through his or her imagination is a child's way of working on a dream. The ability to reenter a dream and allow it to develop through active imagination is a critical step in dreamwork, one that Western adults need to train in. Here, however, the account goes beyond "report" and is called "dream development."

Once in a while, children may want to keep a dream or part of a dream to themselves. These dreams or parts of dreams may clash with what they understand to be socially acceptable. They may also want to protect dreams that are precious to their heart. The daughter of a professor friend of mine woke one morning saying, "I had the most beautiful dream of my life last night, but I'm not gonna tell," and she went on her way, skipping.

The goal of keeping a dream journal with a child is not to keep an exhaustive inventory, but rather to nurture the child's developing relationship with dreams and dream skills that the child will carry over into later life. Keeping a dream journal is also a way of nurturing the creative life within your family and your home. If your son or daughter is not ready to share a dream or part of a dream, drawing the dream instead is an alternative you can offer.

Children can become secretive if they are pressed for dreams by an over-eager parent. Heed your child's secretiveness. This secretiveness may be a sign that you need to step back and reevaluate your approach with your child's dreams. As the guardian of your child's dream journal, your role is to make way for your child's exploration of his or her dreams. A personal agenda of yours that steers away from that purpose can hurt your child's relationship with her or his dream life, and hurt your relationship with your child too. Your child's reactions to your attitudes, if you take them in and redirect your behavior accordingly, can become your best guide for parenting.

As a child winds down from telling a dream, he or she may add some closing remarks, such as "All the colors of this dream were green and yellow." Or the child may reflect on what is on his or her mind after the dream: "I wish I had a sister, someone to play with," or "I don't like my teacher anymore. She has become mean." Closing remarks are valuable fodder for the dream journal and they may invite a heart-to-heart conversation with the child.

Dream Drawing

Not only can toddlers and preschoolers dictate their dreams as parents record them, but they can draw their dreams. And they do so in their journal. When children too work in their journals, it makes the journal their own. Drawing their dreams helps children remember them and think about them.

Once you have started recording your child's dreams, make room for your daughter or son to illustrate them. Look for a spontaneous moment to invite your child, "Would you like to draw the witch," or "Would you like to draw your dream?" Gratifying a young child's interest on the spur of the moment is usually the most successful approach. So you can pass your child the pen you were using to record the dream. Before you know it, your child will be at work drawing the dream witch and other elements from the dream.

Dream journaling becomes an occasion for precious time together, usually in the morning before the day takes off. With kindergarten-aged children, dream drawing occurs more frequently. In the quiet of your day, make room for dream drawing with your child. Dreams can bring forth a creative spirit that will touch both you and your child. When you work side by side with your child—your child drawing his or her dream, you working on something else—a sense of closeness, a bond, emerges between the two of you as a result of this sharing of common creative space.

Your young dreamer may prefer a dream journal or separate sheets of paper, which you can keep in a special sheath. Children use anything from pencil and pens to crayons and felt pens to draw their dreams. Occasionally, dreams and attention spans merit special art materials such as watercolors or glitter pens. The energy of the dream itself will focus your child's attention when drawing a dream.

Dream drawing is hard work, and it is unrealistic to expect children to make a drawing every time they tell a dream, or to make a complete picture each time they draw a dream. Do not try to force this, or it will quickly become unappealing. It is much better to let the process unfold organically as "fun." Children may draw their dreams only from time to time, but even so, their drawings add dimension to a child's dream journal.

Young children's drawings are at first rudimentary but keep pace with their developing motor skills. Gradually, their ability to represent the images of their dreams increases. Looking back, they may gaze with delight on a doodle that is incomprehensible to others and know exactly what it represents.

Children portray the essential features of the dream. Some dream drawings focus only on the dream location. Others depict the main characters. Drawings that integrate both are actually fairly sophisticated. Some dream illustrations are no bigger than a sand dollar, while others fill up a whole page. I have seen dreams "staged" within a rectangle, the rectangle representing a room or house. For example, the rectangle might be the outline of a pet shop, within which the viewer sees animals in their pens and cages. Sometimes drawings show the interplay of characters. A little girl named Elizabeth, who had probably seen such things in comics, drew her characters with word bubbles and asked her father to help her with the words.

Remember, your child's expression is his or hers alone. The images and words do not have to make sense to you. If the word bubble says something silly (I have read, for instance, "A silly Fred with lots of tears and only a head"), just go with it. Adult dreams often do not add up easily either.

Some dream drawings portray the dreamer in his or her bed with the dream next to the dreamer. Six-year-old Steven drew himself lying on top of his bunk bed dreaming. In a large bubble pointing to his head, Steven drew his dream. The drawing depicts a big boy, Martin, pushing a little boy who falls with his face against the cement, bleeding. A witness to the scene, Steven, yells at Martin, "STOP!" This brings about a reversal in the dream, when unexpectedly Martin congratulates Steven for telling him to stop. In the drawing, Steven represents the two scenes—Martin pushing the boy and congratulating dream Steven—in one single image. On the left of the picture, we see Martin pushing the boy with his two hands; on the right side, he is also congratulating Steven with a third hand. Steven is standing underneath a stop sign.

I have found that dreams and drawings of dreams do not always match each other in intensity. A child might merely sketch a powerful dream but spend a long time on a dream that seems less consequential. That latter dream's features might become more apparent through the qualities of its drawing.

A few drawings stand out because of the brightness of their colors and the power of their images. Some are richly detailed. Some still vibrate with the emotion of the dream. Key, however, is the weight the child attaches to the dream, not your involvement.

Dream Scribblers

Children who see an adult thoughtfully recording dreams might have the impulse to write their dreams too, if only by imitation at first. Obviously, setting an example entices interest, not just in dreams, but also in writing words. Even though youngsters cannot really write in a formal way, they can put scribbles on paper that stand for a description of their dream. If your child wants to "write" his or her dreams in the journal, give your child the opportunity. Looking back at your son's or daughter's dream journal, you might find the first wavering and unbroken lines of a beginner at three, four, and four and a half. Gradually, these become discrete scribbles, then letters and simple words, as your child's awareness that words are made of letters grows.

When watching an adult write down the whole dream on paper, a child may get inspired to try his or her hand at "spelling" a word or two from the dream. The child might even direct the adult to write a word from the dream in capital letters or with exclamation marks to convey dramatic intensity, as in:

❋ *It was an EMERGENCY!*

❋ *The FIREMEN came!*

❋ *THE CROWN WAS GONE!*

If your child offers you the "spelling" for a word or directs you to write a word or a phrase in a specific way, welcome your child's involvement with the journal. Your child is learning the ropes of writing.

A few years ago, through a common friend, I met a woman who was a creative-writing teacher. She also taught dreamwork to women in prison. When I told her of my children's dream project, she said that her seven-year-old daughter kept a dream journal. Both the girl and the mother agreed to send me the journal. That precious dream journal contained thirteen dreams. There were witch and tidal wave dreams, dreams of falling, of water snakes, and of princesses. The spelling and punctuation were those of a seven-year-old learning how to write. The dream telling, however, was expressive, and the style and rhythm were those of a child gifted in language. Some letters were enlarged as a means of indicating emphasis, "I gave Trudy THE BABY and walked AWAY!"

By the time youngsters can write with fluency, the ability to report their dreams verbally is probably quite advanced and will remain ahead of their ability to write for a long time. As we all know, writing is hard work for young children. Although a nine-year-old can dictate a two-page-long dream, a child that age may shy away from writing her or his dream because "it is too long and too complicated."

Keeping a dream journal with a child encourages the child to learn to write, beginning with dream scribbling, then dream writing, and, eventually, expressive writing. When parents tell me that their child has difficulty with writing, I suggest that their child begin writing his or her dreams. I know that the dream material, because it appeals to the senses and to the feelings, will attune these kids to their creative spirit and free their pen.

Dream scribbling and the first rudiments of dream writing establish a foundation for communication through the written word that will carry over into school and adult life.

The dreams of childhood last only the time of a season. We need to harvest them when they bloom. Be a parent who listens keenly, attention rapt, as your children report on nighttime adventures. It is a temptation to discount or trivialize what they are telling you as "just a dream," particularly if you are busy or the dream is troubling. Yet, as you know from the previous pages, doing so is unwise. You will be, in a sense, robbing your child of respect for his or her unconscious and imagination. You will erode your child's trust in your ability to listen thoughtfully. You are also throwing away an exceedingly valuable opportunity for relationship building.

How much better to "get into it!" Let your mind and

heart travel into the world your child describes. Try to experience the dreams as your son or daughter describes them. I know from my profession and research and from personal experience just how rich this experience can be. You will find that once children tap into their dream source, dreams flow abundantly in a life-giving way.

The door to your child's world of dreams has opened. From now on, your child can become an active dreamer.

CHAPTER FOUR

WHAT DO CHILDREN DREAM ABOUT?

Through your child's dreams, you become a witness to how a child develops day by day, experience by experience, cognitively, socially, physically, emotionally, and spiritually. For help with your reflections as a parent witnessing your child's development, I have arranged the contents of children's dreams according to areas of child development that may be relevant. These include adventures, relationships, the child's body, transitions, and soul.

When you first begin archiving your child's dreams, you may not see much more than an unrelated hodgepodge. As you take a deeper look, however, themes emerge that correspond to areas of child growth and development. Whereas your child's dreams are distinctive, reflecting his or her own truth and beauty, they also correspond to common hopes, challenges, difficulties, friendships, and transitions that all children face. Noting

these will help you as you surf the night's sea of dreams
with your young dreamer.

Going on Dream Adventures:
Heroes and Heroines, Deeds and Medals

The most frequent theme in a child's dreams is
adventure. Life can be compared to a journey with its
myriad challenges, both large and small. Dreams of
adventures reflect those challenges, with the opportunity for the child dreamer to tap into his or her inner
resources to meet them creatively and with a growing
awareness.

Dreams of adventure call a child to new frontiers,
whether in the child's home, in the neighborhood, on a
field trip with the school, or on a visit at the park with the
family . . . anywhere! In these settings appear dark figures, dragons, and dinosaurs. These and other dangers
challenge the child dreamer to feel and overcome whatever apprehensions and fear they trigger.

For each dream adventure, a child may escape the
danger or enemy, or engage in a struggle to overcome the
danger or enemy. These dreams of adventure portray
characteristic steps of a classic heroic quest: the departure for the adventure, the encounter with a danger or an
enemy of sorts, the struggle for a resolution, and the
return home. Sometimes rejoicing and recognition follow
victory. In the dreams, your child demonstrates that he
or she is a hero or a heroine in the making.

In the following dream of adventure, fear turns into
excitement and danger turns into opportunity. When her

adventure begins, Joy (7:6) is on her way to a camping trip with her pal Bob and his mom, Ann:

> Once I was going with Bob and Ann out camping on the beach. And we saw a pirate on the way and that pirate looked calm and gentle. But he was just trying to capture us and put us on a ship. He came to us. While we followed him, his teeth turned into pokers and his fingernails turned into jewels. On one hand was a hook. I whispered to Bob, "Captain Hook! We can meet Peter Pan on this ship. Follow him. We will get good luck." Bob passed that on to Ann, and Ann agreed. So we kept following him. When we reached the ship, we saw Peter Pan. Bob and I both yelled, "Put some fairy dust on us, so we can fly away for ever, with Ann Duncan very far away." Peter Pan said, "Oh just a minute." With one hand he fought with a sword, with the other he put some fairy dust on us and we flew away. When we got to our camping ground, Bob did not want to camp anymore. I wanted to. We went home. Hook was there, and it started all over again.

You may recognize some of the elements of the hero's journey: the departure for the adventure (we were going to camp on the beach), an encounter (we saw a pirate, who turns into Hook), the struggle for a resolution (culminating with the flying), and the return home.

As the preceding dream exemplifies, a dream adventure can be pleasurable and playful. Parents must not lose track of this. The similarities between dreaming and play are worth noting. In the same way that a child's play fosters his or her cognitive development, so does dreaming.

Play is a way to use one's imagination for its own sake. Dreaming is too. Alan Siegel and Kelly Bulkeley stress dreaming as play in the following way:

> Actually, the connection between dreaming and play is surprisingly strong. Researchers who have studied dreaming and play behaviors in humans and other animal species have found that play is autotelic—that is, it is carried out for its own sake, without being directed toward or motivated by any exterior goals. Play involves the creation of an "unreal" or "quasi-real" space, a special area clearly set apart from nonplay reality by special signals and rules. As a result, play is relatively "safe," in that play acts do not have the same consequences that similar acts would have outside of the play space. Researchers have concluded that the primary function of play is to enable us to experiment with different possibilities in our lives, promoting our general flexibility, creativity, and capacity to react well to novel experiences.

> These characteristics of play perfectly describe the activity of dreaming as well. Like play, dreaming is autotelic in the sense of being a self-contained, non-goal-oriented activity . . . In the exact same way, parents should welcome the playful creations of their children's dreams with the same open, non-interpretative attitude, admiring and celebrating these imaginative wonders without making disruptive analyses and interpretations of what the parents think the dreams "really mean."[1]

Your dreaming child is playing, developing his or her creative mind and learning to react to novel situations.

Dreamguiding gives you the opportunity to enjoy your own children's dream adventures.

Like Joy's dream, dreams of adventure frequently feature references to characters from children's literature, television, and films. Princess Jasmine, Ninja Turtles, Aslan, the Three Little Pigs, superheroes, Peter Pan, and Winnie-the-Pooh, all appear in turn in the dreams of children. Children relate to the characters from children's literature and other media, not as separate, but as if they were their peers and friends. "I was riding my bike with Charles," dreams Annie (6:3). "We went somewhere. Charles was looking for a house, and I saw a door. I opened it. Do you know what I saw? Winnie-the-Pooh and all the others. It gave me a good surprise."

The stories, movies, games, and programs resonate with children because the plots reflect challenges with which they themselves struggle, and because they demonstrate how to resolve those challenges.

Having experienced literary children's response to villains, real children can measure themselves against the Captain Hooks, Miss Hannigans, Miss Minchins, and Dolores Umbridges of their dreams, where they rebel against abuse of power on their own. When she was about seven, Hyacinthe dreamt about Miss Minchin, the mean mistress in *The Little Princess,* and she stood up to her:

> The mean mistress, Miss Minchin, was teaching school in the kitchen. She told us to recite the alphabet. I don't know why, but I was the only one in the kitchen, and I said "No." Then she told me to copy all the pages of the dictionary. I said "No" again. She spanked me. I was screaming in my dream.

If dreaming is an occasion for play and the development of the creative mind, dreams like Hyacinthe's
demonstrate that it is also an opportunity for the child to
develop her or his ego strength. Through these adventures, the child is stimulated to become centered, as well
as to mobilize his or her strength as it is experienced.

Dreams of adventure can turn into nightmares when
they involve a dreadful encounter, too scary for the child to
cope with. Here is how it began for preschooler Eddie (5:0):

> My dream was scary. We were in McDonald's. We
> climbed up the McClimber and I went into a hole and
> opened the door. Everything was white. I opened another
> door. There were birds standing. They looked like fight-
> ing birds. Then I opened another door and I was out.

Fortunately for Eddie, the ride allowed him to be out
in no time.

Michelle's (11:4) adventure, on the other hand, turns
to full-fledged nightmare, when the bottom of the pool
begins cracking and a shark appears:

> I was in a pool and the concrete at the bottom started
> cracking and there was a shark in there. I got out and I
> had a ship. And so I went in it. (For a second I knew that
> I was in a dream and I said, "Michelle, wake up!" I
> couldn't wake up.) And so, I ran all the way to my aunt's
> house and I locked the door. And then there is a shelf. I
> dropped it and it went swirling on the floor. And I was on
> the floor and I changed into a dog. I was trying to get
> away from the shark, 'cause all of a sudden, all the
> cement started breaking. The water was spreading out
> and the shark was beginning to follow. And I woke up.

Michelle was a "black tall dog," she told me, "a big-size dog." In order to get away from the shark breaking through the floor of the pool, Michelle first got out of the pool and boarded her ship. (She even tried, unsuccessfully, to wake herself up from the dream.) When she eventually changed into a dog, as a dog, she was still running away from the advancing water and shark. (Michelle is connected to dogs and has two.) The water in a pool is contained water. As the cement of the pool begins to crack open, water can flow unhindered. This unbound water is home to a devouring sea creature threatening Michelle in her dream. Michelle got away by waking up.

Matters of the Heart: Playmates and Friends, Love, Teachers, and Pets

Matters of the heart are a primary dynamic in everyone's life, including every child's life. Although each of us and each child rely daily on an exchange of emotional sustenance, somehow the development of emotions takes the back seat to "performance" in the Western world. In the mid-1990s, the phrase "emotional intelligence" was popularized to account for these skills that are so important in life yet are not the object of formal instruction. Dreams are the terrain *par excellence* for emotional intelligence. In dreams we foster its development, no matter our age.

Matters of the heart begin with parental love. In this section, I focus on peers, romance, teachers, and pets, and I reserve for chapter 9 the subject of parental images in children's dreams.

Playmates and Siblings

Children grow in relation to other children and they develop social skills through interacting with kids their age. Their dreams portray a large array of situations involving playmates. Most of the time, playmates share the dreamer's activity, play, or adventure in the dream. But the dreams also put the struggles of socialization with peers and with siblings into focus. Children dream that children near their own age take their toys away, trick, and attack them. Four-year-old Erin dreamt of her sister:

> We were playing blocks, and I was building a tower, but my sister kept breaking it. I said no, but she kept breaking it.

If children's dreams provide a window on children's social struggles, they also show that children have the resources to fare socially, to solve problems, and to work out compromises. In dreams, children practice and develop social skills, as well as work out dilemmas they face in their individual lives.

While children interact with a large array of playmates throughout their days, at school, and in the neighborhood, they establish bonds with special friends early on and these special friends are featured in their dreams. Five-year-old Judy dreams of finding the perfect birthday gift for her friend Alice. In the dream, she anticipates Alice's delight at receiving her gift:

> I found this ballerina box and I found a ballerina and I told the storekeeper to fix it and I took it home

and it was Alice's birthday tomorrow. So I wrapped it with wrapping paper. I gave her the ballerina set with the drawer at the bottom and a ballerina and the medium-sized hole at the bottom and a ring compartment. Alice was so happy!

Hearing a dream like this from your child gives you the opportunity to rejoice over their relationships too.

The best of friends can also cause pain to each other without consciously intending it. Peter (5:8), whose bullet dream I mentioned in chapter 2, hurt his friend in a dream. The retaliation from his friend's father was dreadful. Yet, through an amazing turn of events in the dream, Peter got off scot-free:

> I was walking with my friend Frank and I hurt him. He went to tell his father. Then he [the father] shot me with a bullet and it bounced on me. It became all flat and it fell on the ground. Frank said: "Are you bionic?" Then, the dream was over.

In the dream drawing, we see Peter and Frank together, then Frank going away crying, Frank's father with his gun, and again Peter with the bullet smashed against his chest. The father is mad enough at Peter to shoot him. The intensity of the father's anger may reflect Peter's perception of Frank's dad's character. But it may also mirror the intensity of Peter's inner turmoil for having hurt Frank and his worst fear of what might come out of it. At the end of the dream, however, Frank is awed by what he saw, and balance is restored. The chest, against which the bullet gets smashed, being the center for the heart, suggests the power of the heart.

Children dream of being alienated from their friends at times, but they also dream of the joy of making up. When children are separated from their best friends because of distance, they sometimes visit them in a dream. An encounter with a friend in a child's dream can be real to the point that the child may wake up from a dream in tears, when he or she realizes that the friend who had been so close in the dream is still thousands of miles away.

A Touch of Romance

Your child's dreams sometimes reflect a touch of romance. Children's dreams show that children can be visited by feelings of being "in love" early on. Parents should not be surprised if their first grader wakes up one day saying, "I dreamt that I lost two teeth, that I was in love, and that I lived in the same house but with different parents." Children's dreams of love may include hugs and kisses, being a bride, having a lover, and being loved.

Teachers on Our Children's Path

Before long, your young child will be in the care of adults outside your home. Teachers can have a significant effect in the lives of children and can inspire them to give their best. Some teachers have a way of making each pupil feel loved and recognized. This heartfelt acknowledgment gives children wings. Approval by people outside their family builds self-confidence and a feeling of possibilities.

Even though school-age children spend thirty hours a week receiving academic instructions from teachers, schoolwork does not figure prominently in their dreams. This is because waking life experience is not represented in dreams on the basis of the frequency of its occurrence, but on the basis of its interest and meaning for the child.[2] On the other hand, children dream of having their work chosen by teachers and of going on field trips with teachers. Children dream of school parties from preschool on. They dream of having their birthdays marked on the class calendar and celebrated at school. These activities are portrayed in children's dreams because they hold value and meaning for a child.

As they move along the school track, children leave their teachers behind. Maria's (6:1) dream captures a moment of passage in her young life as she watches her former kindergarten teacher with her new class:

> I was riding my bike on the street here. I saw Mrs. E. walking along on a field trip to the pool. She was with her new class. The class was smaller. Mrs. E. joked to me, "Wanna be in my new class?" I had already been in her class. I walked with them all the way to the end of the street. She held my hand.

In addition to schoolteachers, children have sports coaches and teachers of art, drama, voice, and dance. Children learn to cope with adults whose personalities may be a challenge to them. Children feel stress at times from school and their relationships with teachers, and their dreams reflect this. In a dream, a witch is loose in the classroom, or the dream points to a child's hurt and angry feelings at a teacher's unfairness, as in ten-year-old Kerry's dream, reported in Ann Sayre Wiseman's *Nightmare Help:*

A Guide for Parents and Teachers.[3] In his dream, Kerry sees his teacher die in a car explosion:

> This guy was whipping me. He stole a car; it hit a rock and exploded. He died. I was scared because it was really Rob, my gym teacher.

In the dream, Kerry is subjected to his teacher's abuse. The whipping is an image for how Kerry feels treated by his teacher, whom he characterizes as being "like a sergeant." The dream teacher also shows himself to be a thief who steals a car—a fancy car, we learn, as Kerry adds, "He had this really fancy car." What leaves Kerry deeply troubled in the end, however, is the unexpected and deadly outcome of the dream when the car accidentally hits a rock and the teacher explodes. "But a dream like this really scares me," said Kerry, "because he was killed. I saw him explode. It was like it really happened, like I MADE IT HAPPEN."

With the help of his dream guide, Kerry came to understand the explosion in the dream as an image for his feeling of anger. "I explode easily when I'm mad," he acknowledged. Prompted by his guide, Kerry explored alternative endings to the dream that would leave him feeling more comfortable inside. First, he envisioned Rob being fired by the principal, then whipped by the army (a repeat of what he did not like to receive from Rob). Then it occurred to him that perhaps Rob's parents whipped him as a child and that this was what "made him mean." This opened a door for Kerry to begin understanding his teacher, which, he found, made him feel better: "I guess it will feel better in the end if I can understand him."

Communicating about a dream with a child is part of the value of dreamguiding. When your child is experiencing difficulty with a teacher, giving your child support begins with acknowledging his or her experience and feelings about it.

Pets

Children's matters of the heart include relationships with pets. Children have a special kinship with animals, who, like children, are vulnerable and require tending. Having a pet is, in many ways, an early occasion for a child to learn responsibility.

Those for whom having a pet is a deep heart's desire dream of receiving a pet as a birthday gift, of finding a pet in the forest, or of choosing a pet at the shelter. Those who have pets and are emotionally bonded to them dream of their pets as companions in adventure. They also dream of their pets when they are hurt and when they lose them, either because they ran away or because they die.

The force of a child's feeling for a pet comes through in the next dream. After the death of IFR, the family cat, Paul (3:8) was on a walk with his dad one day when they found a bone, "This must be the bone of a dead animal," Paul's dad noted, as he picked up the bone.

"Where are the bones of IFR?" asked Paul, beginning to cry. That night Paul had his first dream:

> I saw IFR in my nap. He was standing up and talking on the phone with my grand-maman. He had hands and feet.

The dream portrays a cat with human features able to talk on the phone with the grandmother, as Paul usually did with his grandmother. The dream integrates in one image the child and his beloved pet as if Paul and his cat were one.

A glimmer of new life may come through a child's dream, beyond the grieving period following the loss of a pet. Several months after the family bunny had escaped from under the fence, Judy dreamt of a cake made of a real bunny that comes to life. She put the new bunny in her old pet's cage:

> Well, we went to the pet shop, and the pet keeper gave us a cake made out of a real live bunny. Then I tasted a little bit of the bottom, and I ate all the icing off the top, and then I took it home and it came alive and I put it in Fluffytails' cage where Fluffytails used to live. And it was a little baby white one that hopped on top of all the black and white ones.

Occasionally, children's pets happen to drown in dreams or be hurt by an adult, known or unknown to the child. How adults treat pets influences children's young hearts because children identify with their pets.

The Body: Food, Physical Prowess, Injuries, Nudity, and Teeth

Your child's body is his or her life conveyance. Although conveyances in dreams can be images for the dreamer's ego, they can also be images for the dreamer's body. Children's physical health is of primary concern to

every parent. Children's physical well-being and growth
enter their dream life.

Bodily Functions

Elimination becomes fodder for dream life at all ages
because it is so much a matter of control and is
entrenched in feelings of privacy and shame. Very young
children dream about being potty trained. Curt (3:6)
dreamt that he had three pee-pees. Bed-wetting dreams
and dreams of letting go while waiting in line or outdoors
may be prompted by the sensation of a full bladder or a
full bowel during sleep. These dreams may also coincide
with a release of energy, a letting go of tension, or a reconnecting with one's instincts.

Food and Candy

Food is an object of exploration and discovery in children's dreams. Young children dream of eating simple
foods, like an egg or a tomato. Older children dream of
eating special foods, like lobster and shrimp. Children of
all ages dream of the thrill of the candy store, of ice
cream, chocolate, and cookies.

In his dream, Jimmy (3:8) has never had a tomato and
he wants to taste one. But his friend tricks him into eating a cucumber instead:

> The big boys had the tomatoes, but I didn't get
> one. I never had one before so I decided that I wanted
> to taste one. Yasir snatched a tomato from Najam and
> he gave it to me, but it was really a cucumber instead.
> That was a very bad joke to play on me. And I told
> my mama. That was all. There were no more dreams.

As shown in Jimmy's dream, food soon becomes a commodity for power among children. Young children often dream of having food taken away from them. Sometimes it is an animal that takes food from the child and sometimes an adult, but most often it is a peer of the child.

Children also dream of sharing food with their friends. Seven-year-old Erika dreams of sharing her breakfast plate with a friend. The image suggests a close relationship between the girls and a cause for envy in a third person, Jan. This is Erika's written account of her dream:

> "Martha," I asked, "you want my breakfast?"
> "Sure," said Martha. She ate it.
> Jan gasped, "You guys were sharing plates!"

As children's imagination expands, food images become intermingled in dreams of adventure. In these dreams, children are sometimes confronted with evil-doers who use food as a weapon. Mirroring a theme common in fairy tales, as with the evil queen and her poisoned apple in Snow White, dream food turns to threat in the hands of a witch or bad guys. There is soap in the food, a witch inflicts her poison on the child's pet, or a villain wants to compel the dreamer to eat something against his or her will. Depending on the experience of the child, these themes might address children's wariness about trusting something or someone that seems nurturing.

Whatever the circumstance, fascination with food, procuring it, hoarding it, eating it, and celebrating with it are important childhood dream themes that reflect a healthy interest in self-nurturing.

Prowess and Performance

Children develop new physical powers and capabilities at every stage of their development. Children measure their growth by the prowess they demonstrate. Performing well in a dream is just as glorious, Here is Audrey's (4:10) dream:

> I have a beautiful, beautiful dream. I went to Sea World and there was a swimming pool and I just swim and I was three years old and I knew how to swim up to five, and it was deep.

Dreams of prowess and performance reflect the child's growing confidence in his or her ability to deal with life's challenges. A child may also have a taste in dreams of a capability he or she does not yet have in waking life, announcing a soon-to-be new mastery. For instance, Annie (6:3) reported, "I dreamt that I was able to ride on a two-wheel bicycle, but I can't."

There is a kinesthetic quality to performance dreams, with the felt sense of the experience of the movement itself, as in rollerblading gracefully, for instance. Children dream of counting goals in hockey and other sports. Nine-year-old Sylvia dreamt of winning the Olympics. Children's dreams of performing extend beyond physical prowess. They dream of making it in math, of giving speeches, and of singing and dancing on stage.

Dreams of falling, failing a test, or underperforming

show the other side of the coin. While on vacation with his family, nine-year-old Tommy had a dream following a gymnastics competition:

> I was at a gymnastics competition. I was there and I was going on the trampoline. I was jumping. I did my routine and I fell off the trampoline. But then I fell off and when I was off the trampoline, it was like . . . there was water under the trampoline. Then I ended up in a pool. In the pool, there were a lot of fish. Then I was in an ocean. And when I was in the ocean, my parents were waiting for me on the beach. And then we had lunch.

Before going on vacation, Tommy had his first gymnastics competition and a kid about a year older than he had fallen off the trampoline. In the dream, Tommy is the one who falls. Yet through the grace of the dream there is water to receive him underneath the trampoline. From there he journeys from one body of water to the next. This water, at first indiscriminate, becomes a pool enlivened with fish, and then an ocean from which he emerges to find his parents and lunch waiting for him.

When Tommy told his parents the dream, they were impressed with his adaptive responsibility about his friend's fall. And, of course, they were very happy to be invited into the dream as lunch companions.

Ailments, Injuries, and Hurts

When a child has a dream involving physical discomfort, always listen to the dream carefully and make sure that the child is okay. An emotional hurt can open the door to physical hurt. For example, it is not uncommon that children who have received a blow to their self-esteem are hurt physically soon after. It is also a well-known point of view that diseases can appear in the emotional body before manifesting in the physical body, and can thus be foreseen in dreams. Children's ailments can permeate their dreams. Sometimes the dream is plain: The child who hurt his foot dreams of having hurt feet. At other times, as with four-year-old Nooriya, the dream speaks symbolically:

> I had a scary dream, I had a fever. I had a spider
> in my ear. It was stuck there.

Nooriya actually had an earache, but she made her dream spider responsible.

Dreams where children are hurt may symbolize their vulnerability in the area of the body affected. The area of the body attacked in the dream—legs, tummy, neck, face—can give a hint as to the specificity of the vulnerability at stake. If the child is bitten on the foot in the dream and can only walk painfully, the question to ask may be, "Is my child's forward movement impaired right now and by what?" Although only speculative, such a question can open the door to insight into the meaning of the dream.

Another consideration is the *source* of the child's injury in the dream. Is it the result of an accident or of an attack? If an attack, who attacked the child? Is it someone familiar or, as in Lili's dream, a snake?

This was one day my mom went to the mall and she bought two snakes. She didn't know they were rattlesnakes, and she bought them 'cause she is interested in snakes. And she bought a red and black one and a gray snake. They had rattles, but they were on top of the rattles. So she didn't see the rattles. She gave me the black and red one. She got the gray one. I took mine out of the cage and it bit me four times. Then my mom took hers out and it bit her two times. And I cried and I wouldn't stop crying.

According to Jung, dreams of being bitten by a snake are symbolic of the sudden and dangerous action of the instincts upon the psyche. A psychic attack needs to be dealt with. Since the attack is psychic, the healing will be too.

Nudity

Dreams of nudity have a large array of meanings in children's dreams. Nudity is both an expression of exuberant freedom and an image of vulnerability. Being naked or partly naked in public in a child's dream can represent having felt exposed, unprotected, or embarrassed. The child's felt sense is translated into literal terms in the dream.

The humor of going to the bathroom or being without clothes in the wrong place and at the wrong time does not escape even a young child. When children have dreams of intrusion on their privacy, such as "being seen" through the crack of the door of a public bathroom, the dream may point to a related incident of exposure in the child's life. The dream may also be a symbol for a violation of the child's boundaries or sense of self, or the fear of it. The violation of the privacy of one's body in the dream then stands for a violation of the child's self.

Teeth and Braces

One of the most dramatic changes children undergo is losing teeth at the end of early childhood, between the ages of five and seven. It will take six to seven years for all the permanent teeth to be in place and another five to six years for the wisdom teeth to appear. Losing one's baby teeth is impressive to children and they dream of it:

> I dreamt that I had lost two more teeth, two sharp ones over here in the front. (5:6)

Other tooth dreams include getting a loose tooth from cracking something hard with one's teeth, feeling a tooth fall out of one's mouth, and putting a tooth under one's pillow for the tooth fairy to come.

Wearing braces has become a symbol for growing up in our culture. To young children, anticipating orthodontia is so important that braces become a dream subject:

> One day it was Christmas day, and I was sleeping in my bed and Santa Claus brang me some braces. And that day I was so excited that I had braces in my mouth. And I was proudly wearing them with glee. And one day my braces fell out. Santa Claus knew that I had crooked teeth. And then they fell out in my mouth. I could not put them back in, but then I remembered something. My mom could put my braces in my mouth. I went to ask the teacher and she could not put them in. (5:6)

Crossing Thresholds: Death and Rebirth

A child's dreams about crossing major thresholds are easy to miss, even though they point to a significant process in personal development. Development goes in spurts rather than evenly, though each year sees tremendous physical and mental changes. Growing up is marked by the gradual conquest of new territories of autonomy. For a three-year-old, conquering new territory might be walking home by her or himself for the first time. Leaving a teacher behind at six, as in the dream quoted earlier, marks a time of passage. Puberty delivers a whole new set of physical and emotional unknowns. Marked transitions from one phase to another usually come with both gain and a loss of what is left behind. Children experience these gains and losses profoundly and their sometimes-vivid dreams contain images indicating the dramatic transitions.

Even in young children, images of decay and new life, implying endings and new beginnings, may appear in dreams at such times of passage. For example, in June's (8:8) dream, greens grew in her dress-up boxes (boxes full of costumes):

> Mommy told me that when she looked in my dress-up boxes, they were filled with greens. And then I saw the gardeners taking them outside into the compost.

The image of the dress-up boxes filled with greens suggests that they were left behind and that greens grew in them over time. A source of enchantment at an earlier stage of childhood, the dress-up boxes are now left to decompose. As compost, they will serve to fertilize new growth in this eight-year-old psyche. This dream image speaks of those deep growth processes that go unnoticed on the surface.

In seven-year-old Erika's dream, she has the vivid experience of traveling to the unknown:

> I felt myself slide through one tunnel. Then the next thing I knew, I was traveling to another world. I slid out of the tunnel and felt grass growing.

There is a touch of the otherworldly in Erika's dream as she finds herself propelled forward. As a passageway between two worlds, the tunnel suggests death. On the other end, where Erika feels grass growing, is an image of new growth and of new life. Images of death followed by rebirth mark times of passage.

For Ronnie (13:4), it was his dog that crossed to another world. That night he saw a white light in his dream:

> My dog died. I was seven or six. He was really close to us. He had a tumor in his heart. That day that he died, I woke up and I went on the sofa and looked out the window for a while. It was really hard for me. It was the closest family member that actually died. That night I dreamt of a white light, of a bright white light. I never forgot.

Progressing from one stage to the next, children leave the security of familiar grounds to enter new territories, and this progression often registers in dream sequences. Children change not only externally, but in their attitudes and ways of being in the world as well.

Gifts from the Gods: Fairies, Talking Animals, and Special Finds

Gifts from the dream world, small or big, light children's paths during the daytime and at night. Some dreams have a numinous quality. They are imbued with aesthetic, moral, or emotional features, which leave an impression on the dreamer and often on others who hear the dream. A relationship between the ego and the soul begins to develop, then expands, mediated by dream images. (Your child's ego is the part that operates in and responds to the outside world. The soul encompasses inner feelings and the essence of a person.)

Friends unknown in real life may appear in your child's dreams. These beings recognize the child and light his or her way. Some are lifelike, some are angel- and fairy-like beings (a gentle boy with curly hair and bluish skin, a butterfly maiden), and some are gentle animals. Sometimes these dream beings are only a few years older than the child dreamer, as if they were there to model the child's own growth.

The dreamer may take on another form than his or her own, as in nine-year-old Daisy's dream, where she is a fairy among fairies:

I dreamt that I was a fairy. It was near my house. Everything was exactly the way it is in reality (I do not see any of the other houses in the dream). The rest was different. There were rivers and streams. We were being chased by this guy. He had a brown beard and brown hair. He looked like a real man. We could fly, 'cause we were fairies. We flew to my favorite tree.

She later added that there were seven fairies, but that she could see only her best-friend fairy, which had a blue face and blue wings, long blond hair, and a purple dress. Although she could not see them, she could "hear the other fairies' wings."

Some dreams portray a spiritual hero: a religious figure, an Indian chief or princess, or Aslan (the lion from *The Chronicles of Narnia* by C. S. Lewis). Some include memorable and mysterious symbols that can be images for the soul: an animal endowed with special power, a child, a tree, a garden, a precious stone, a hidden treasure. These dreams go beyond the child's ego to instill hope and faith. Some dreams come in the form of lucky finds, such as precious stones, rocks, or baby chicks. The dreamer discovers something in the dream. Such dreams feel like gifts from the gods.

With my assurances that these themes are common and constructive, I urge you to encourage your child's dreams. Children's dreams reflect and intertwine with their daily lives. Even when disturbing, dreams carry your child to emotional safety by way of hopes, challenges, difficulties, and relationships—all played out under the blankets and under the stars.

PREPARING CHILDREN
FOR THE NIGHT

As every parent knows, bedtime rituals help smooth the passage from dusk until dawn. Though children may grumble over needing to go to bed, most come to enjoy the rituals of teeth brushing and bath, fresh pajamas or nightgown, back rub, cradlesongs, and stories as part of their departure into sleep. Comforting routines make the send-off into the starry night one of tranquility, so that child and parents can rest secure in one another and in the respect they bear for the dreams that may come.

Early Evening Play

Sometimes the first step is early evening play, a joyous prelude to a family's bedtime ritual. Who does not remember playing with siblings before bed? Using sofa cushions strewn about the floor, we jumped from one "rock" to another without falling "into the water." The best part of the game was when everyone ended up falling on each other. There is deep joy in play, when kids exert themselves and join in a happy frenzy.

When little Ruth played hide-and-seek with her family in the early evening, she delighted in hiding in hard-to-find places. Small as she was, she could slip into a laundry basket or a drawer, so no one, to her great delight, could find her. As a preschooler playing horsey with her dad, Mimi would train her horse with different commands for going forward, stopping, rising up, and bowing. And of course, her "horse" would deliberately disobey the commands, which led to falls and much laughter. Playing horsey generated even more excitement when Mimi's friend Justin stayed at her house and they both took turns astride her father. Such energetic games release tension with hilarity before quieting down for bedtime rituals. The results are deeply relaxing.

Contrast this with the more common convention of watching television before bedtime. Much depends on the programming. Television can feed pleasant dreams or nightmares, but suffice it to say that it does "feed." When children go directly from television or video games to bed, they carry a head full of images and ideas that may disserve their dreams. Better to have a quiet time, without such stimulation. My opinion, and experience, is that watching television, a passive occupation, does not reinforce camaraderie, as do reading together, playing cards or board games, and roughhousing.

Warm Sudsy Baths and Dream Costumes

For most, the first steps toward sleep are by way of teeth brushing and warm sudsy baths. These activities teach children to tend to themselves. They are relaxing and soothing. Fred, at fifty-nine, still remembers his bedtime bath ritual. "This is a work bath, son," his father would say. "We knew that this was not a play bath," recalls Fred. "Play bath involved ducks and boats and splashing. My father meant short and to the point." One evening at Veronica's house, the traditional bath ritual took a whole other turn when a visiting uncle squirted shaving cream into the children's bath water. The kids played in the white foam up to their necks as if in clouds. That was play bath. Whether leisurely or speedy, bathing renews your child and prepares him or her for the night and its dream adventures. Out of the bath and into pajamas a child goes. Clean, warm, and comfortable pajamas and nightgowns that appeal to children's fantasies are dream costumes.

The Dream Chamber

A child's bedroom should be a safe haven. Not only is it the place to return to for rest and restoration at the end of the day, it is the only place in the house that is a child's. It is also the child's dream chamber.

If the bedroom is the dream craft, then a special bed with sheets chosen by parent and child together, warm blankets, fluffy comforter, and soft pillows are components that make the pilot seat. Your child will rub his or her fingers over those linens and remember the feel for a lifetime. Best of all, bed covers are made especially for the dream vessel and the bed is made with love. What girl would not want a *ciel-de-lit* (canopy) over her bed to sail the realms of her dreams?

Together, you and your child can make a dream catcher, in the Native American tradition, which you can hang together. Hung above the bed, the dream catcher is a net woven around a wooden ring, which is then decorated with feathers and beads. The dream catcher is believed to protect the dreamer from bad dreams by catching them in its magic web while letting good ones through the hole in its middle.

Why not plan together to add dream features to the room: a starry ceiling, billowing curtains that serve as dream-filled sails for traveling into the night, a nightlight, a favorite blanket, talismans or protective figures to ward off irksome dream characters, and, of course, the dream journal. In antiquity, a god piercing a "demon of the night" was painted on the bed's headboard.

Adjust the room's ambiance to help your child let go of anxiety and become more tranquil: soft lighting, an ordered room, and a closed closet door so no monster can hide in there. Ward off extraneous noise entering the room from loud television or from a big sister's new music. We know from research that light stimulates wakefulness. If you are reading together, focus the light only on the book being read.

Sharing the Magic Hour

Magic threads through the air in the hours and minutes prior to a child falling asleep. Conjure the moment. This magic runs through your fingers at times when you rub or rock your child to sleep. Ballads and lullabies you heard as a child may bubble to the surface, inspiring you to hum tunes that were meaningful to you as a youngster. Memories of your past and your child's past may spring to life when your child asks, "Tell me a story of when you were little" and as he or she grows older, "Tell me a story of when I was little." Set this time aside. Set everything else aside, including all electronic and digital devices.

In *Everyday Blessings,* Myla Kabat-Zinn tells about both the challenges and the rewards of being "present" to a child at bedtime:

> As hard as we both try to protect this time, many things get in our way. Work to be done, phone calls to make, arrangements for the next day, more than one child needing us, or children of different ages having different needs, often pulling us in different directions. Older children's needs often get shortchanged, taking a back seat to the younger ones'. It's an ongoing juggling act. Sometimes a peaceful bedtime gets lost in all this. But the nights when I make the physical and psychic space to be fully present and somehow it comes about, sharing a child's concern or feeling her drift into sleep with her head on my chest, I am reminded of how precious this time can be.[1]

Little girls and boys, lying in bed at the end of the day, may have sudden access to the aches and pains they have been ignoring all day. As the night draws near, they also get in touch with hurt feelings in need of repair. Iron things out with your child before he or she goes to sleep;

talk things over. Or, doing something creative together, you might play a board game, listen to music, be enthralled by the same storybook. These activities relieve the tensions of the day and prepare a child's spirit for a good night of sleep. They release anxieties that might otherwise follow the child into the night.

Bedtime rituals have their place with older kids too. Tucking preteens in is one of the ways of trouble-proofing preadolescents. Parents insist that a bedtime tête-à-tête loosens the tongues of otherwise silent middle schoolers.[2] When your child shares his or her concerns, your emotional availability to the child is significant. Make sure that there is time for your child to complete her or his feeling. Eye contact, a soothing tone of voice, and a warm touch will reflect your emotional presence. Even teenagers still enjoy being read to occasionally, listening to soothing music before drifting off to sleep, and even being tucked in, however briefly.

Stories and Songs

Climbing in bed for storytelling or reading, sometimes with siblings all in one bed, is a treat. Why not use this precious occasion to pass on family stories and give them life? Children love to hear made-up stories or to hear stories about the past.

There is also an extraordinary wealth of children's books available nowadays at bookstores and libraries—not to mention books online and books on tape—making reading to children a task full of choice, delight, beauty, and surprise. A parent who has discovered quality stories with the help of a children's librarian gives a child the best food for slumber in the world. In most of the best children's stories, the parents are removed at the beginning of the story. Then the protagonist can be on her or his own and the adventure begins. For example, in *James and the Giant Peach*, Roald Dahl kills off the parents on the first page. We remember Dorothy with her Aunt Em and Uncle Henry because we don't know where her parents are. But L. Frank Baum has to get rid of her aunt and her uncle for the deeper part of the story to begin. As the pages turn, children enter an imaginary world, treading the path of the heroes and heroines, away from their immediate concerns.

An adult voice reading aloud can be music to a child's heart. My husband remembers, long ago, a UCLA cardiologist named Dr. Lou Zeldis reading *Charlotte's Web* near bedtime to six children with such obvious relish that he has never forgotten his lively tone of voice.

Many agree that soothing rhythmic motions and sounds, such as rocking the cradle, a back rub, nursery rhymes, and lullabies, help little ones nestle into the nighttime. If you play an instrument, play for your child before going to sleep. Or repeat a soothing song by the side of your child's bed every night. Or make it up as you go along. Children will carry these bedtime rituals forward, not just through their childhood dreams, but also into adulthood, as a means of letting go of stress and honoring the nighttime.

Nighttime Companions

Dolls, Action Figures, and Stuffed Animals

In antiquity, children's toys served as charms or amulets to protect them from malevolent influences. In our era of large-scale commercialization of children's toys, being reminded of these old beliefs has the refreshing effect of a return to the source. In fairy tales and legends all over the world and in children's literature, dolls have a role as children's protective companions. In the Russian tale *Vasalisa,* a young mother on her deathbed gives her daughter Vasalisa a small doll as a parting gift. "Here is a doll for you, my love," she says. "Should you lose your way or be in need of help, ask this doll what to do. You will be assisted. Keep the doll with you always. Do not tell anyone about her. Feed her when she is hungry. This is my mother's promise to you, my blessing on you, dear daughter."[3]

In *The Legend of the Blue Bonnet* retold by Tomie de Paola, the heroine's name is She-Who-Is-Alone. Her parents and her grandparents have died in a famine. All that She-Who-Is-Alone has left from her past is her warrior doll, which her late mother made for her. On the doll's head are blue-jay feathers, which her father gave her.[4] Similarly, in Frances Hodgson Burnett's novel *A Little Princess,* Sara's mother died when she was born. Before her father departs for India, he gives Sara a doll as a friend with whom she can talk when she misses him.[5]

In these and other fairy tales and stories, dolls help along the way. When Vasalisa's stepmother and her two daughters, pretending that there is no fire at the house, send Vasalisa to the Baba Yaga to fetch fire, Vasalisa is terrified to have to find her way through the forest. She then turns to her doll to be guided to the Baba Yaga's house. And when she is overwhelmed by the tasks that the Baba Yaga sets before her, the doll helps her complete her tasks. It is She-Who-Is-Alone's sacrifice of her warrior doll, her most valued possession, to the Great Spirits that brings rain and life back to the land, thus saving her people. At the hands of Miss Minchin's tyranny, Sara turns to her doll for solace and to cry out her revolt.

Not that long ago, families slept several to a room, or even in one bed. In traditional cultures, families with young children still sleep together. And in recent years, some families have adopted the family bed as a means of fostering family bonding. But with the rise in the standard of living of the last century and the accompanying decline in birth rate, many children today have the luxury of an individual bedroom. This also means that children in our culture sleep alone. As if tied to some primal urge for togetherness, our children remedy this isolation. With a favorite doll, action figure, or stuffed animal as companion, they venture into the night.

In spite of the large number of dolls and stuffed animals that children receive nowadays, they still hold a special place in children's hearts. Children play with them, however many there are, and they may sleep with different dolls on different nights. Sometimes a child gets attached to a particular doll and may even attribute powers to this companion. At one point, six-year-old Will had the "shark forces," several stuffed fish with fangs and stingers. At another, he clung to the "white ranger" (from the Power Rangers), who soon became so dirty that he called him the "gray ranger."

Going to sleep with their night companions gives children a sense of comfort and safety. We must not forget, with so many objects replaceable, how much children invest in their favorite belongings. That investment is more than familiarity. With their touch, look, smell, and even taste, these objects are rich in sensory associations and also in feeling associations.

Today's parents may not share the ancients' belief about the protective value of dolls and toys for children, but most honor their children's attachments to their love-worn friends. They instinctively tuck a doll or a plush animal in the corner of a baby's crib. They put a young child to sleep with a special doll or teddy bear at the child's side. And when the child is old enough to sleep away from home at a sleepover or a camping trip and the child wants to take along a favorite doll, the parents agree, as if they believe in the magic of dolls, as their elders did.

Of Magical Beings and Guardian Angels

A protective companion of the night can also be an inner figure: a magical being or guardian angel. Fictional figures can provide safety and protection to children and empower them when they travel to the land of dreams.

In some religious traditions, children are raised with the belief in guardian angels. A guardian angel is believed to be near the one it protects at all times and especially at night. Roger Martinez is a therapist and dream teacher from Santa Fe, New Mexico. Roger must have been between two and four years old when his dad first planted the idea of angels in his heart and mind as a means of protection from the nightmares of his childhood. Confronted by the increasing threat of his recurring nightmares, he called upon an angel he called "the white monster" in response to troubles he was having with a "dark monster":

I was being chased either by wolves or by a big dark monster. The wolves would chase me into the house from a meadow west of the house and would stop at whichever boundary was set. If I stopped at the living room door, they could go no farther. If I went farther into the house, whether to my bedroom or the bathroom, and shut that door, they could go no farther. If I went to hide in the tub and closed the shower curtain or hid under my bed behind the draping of the sheets, the wolves could go no farther . . . The dark monster dreams happened interchangeably in time with the wolf dreams. These were also from the same direction and area as the wolf dreams. These got consistently more dramatic as they went on. In the first of these, I went into my aunt's home, which is before our house, and there I was safe. The next one I was able to go to my aunt's home, then I went to my home. Similar to the wolves, the dark monster was able to go just as far as I would stop . . . In the third one, it followed me into my parents' house and asked my brother and my cousin who were playing on the floor in my bedroom if they had seen me. I was below the window . . . They said they hadn't seen me and I was again safe.

The finale of these dreams had similarities to these, with the exception that it didn't chase me. I knew it came from the meadow west of the house; this time it came and stood at my bedroom door. It woke me from my sleep as if it was in waking life waking me. It told me it was going to kill everyone in the world whom I knew, cared for, and loved. I found out my family was all being killed and close friends as well. I knew it would not stop there and go on to kill everyone in the world.

That's when I was able to call the white monster—I knew it was an angel. He came to my doorway, the same place where the dark monster stood. I told him what had happened and what would happen. He went out to search for the dark monster and then brought him back to fight him in my parents' living room. I went to the corner of the hallway where I could see them fight. This went on for a long time. I was in my room again when the white monster came back to my room and told me he had killed the dark monster and I would not ever have to worry about him. I asked him about my family, friends, and the people of the world. He told me, "They are all okay and safe."

The nightmares stopped then, never to return. But the angels remained. To this day, their presence continues to develop in Roger's life and in his dreams:

All those nightmares that I had stopped then, so far never to return, and since then the angels have helped in different ways. For the last several years I have had a white dog protecting me in dreams. And about a year ago an angel with wings came and gave me a gift. I took it, not asking or needing to know what it was, but was happy to know that it was a gift from the angel.

Innovative therapists, teachers, and parents invent all kinds of "dream equipment" to help families make it through the night. For instance, a dream teacher from Montréal, Nicole Gratton, developed a self-aid kit for young children struggling with nightmares. The kit includes a secret box with five magic tools: a potion, a secret whistle, magic wings, an anti-monster weapon, and an enchanted key. The kit also includes five magic allies: an elf, a protective angel, a magician, a musician, and a doctor. Each tool and each ally is represented on a card like a game card. Children learn to use these tools and can call upon these allies when needing help in a dream. Some children go to sleep with the card of their favorite tool or ally under their pillow as a means of protection against their recurring bad dreams and nightmares.[6]

Prayers

Your child's loving regard for people, animals, and plants expands his or her heart, no matter the child's age. Evoking a sense of spiritual communion with the world and its beings also brings the comfort of knowing that one is part of and interconnected with a larger whole. Young children feel a particular kinship with animals. This mother's invocation to sleep to her three-year-old daughter in *Winged Pharaoh*, a novel by Joan Grant, appeals to this kinship:

Sleep my daughter.
For the sun has drawn the curtains of the night,
Leaving the stars to watch you while you rest.
The sails of all the river boats are furled,
And birds have folded their far-flying wings.
Lion cubs are sleeping in their mother's warmth,
And fish dream in the shelter of the reeds.
The flowers breathe out their perfume on the dusk,
And all is still, save the night-singing bird.
So sleep, my daughter, and close your drowsy lids
Sleep with the world and let your spirit free.[7]

Every religious tradition has prayers, some sung, for a child's bedtime, which help the child feel protection and security about his or her place in the universe. Here are the lyrics of one such prayer song:

> *F*ather we thank thee for the night
> *And for the pleasant morning light*
> *For rest and food and loving care*
> *And all that makes the world so fair*
> *Help us to do the things we should*
> *To be to others kind and good*
> *In all we do in work or play*
> *To grow more loving every day*

Some parents invite their children to reflect on their own blessings and concerns at prayer time. Some parents make their own prayers, naming all the people who love the child—grandparents, other relatives, and family friends. Or they invite blessings for those for whom the child cares—family members, a sick horse, a friend. Your child can be part of this prayer making, repeating the words with you or inventing some of his or her own. Bedtime rituals evolve over time as children grow.

The Good Night

The most important aspects of bedtime rituals are *contact* and *time*. Take a half hour (or more) to indulge in your loved one, to send him or her off into the night with good wishes such as "Sleep well," "Sleep like an angel," and "See you tomorrow" or with a closing rhyme such as "Sleep tight, don't let the bedbugs bite." This does as much to guard against bad dreams and nightmares, the old "demons of the night," as any other prescription. Being tucked in with a favorite doll or sensing the protection of a spiritual being prepares a child's heart for a peaceful journey. Your little child can surrender to the night, feeling loved and made safe, ready for the adventure of dreams.

CHAPTER SIX

A Child's First Ally
When Facing Bad Dreams
and Nightmares

Nearly every household with young children has, at one time or another, been rocked by nightmares. Panic and seeming irrationality can take over when a young person's slumber is jarred by fright, and that fright is sometimes so untrammeled that it awakens everyone and lingers on not just for a night, but for days and days. Terry's six-year-old son had a monster nightmare so vivid that he insisted that they vacate the house, *that minute*. Hysterical, he tried to drag the dog and her out of the house in the middle of the night and, for weeks afterward, had trouble sleeping unperturbed. Such nightmares send parents scurrying to the pediatrician, to the child psychologist, and to bookshelves and the Internet.

For the next couple of days, with anxiety at a pitch,

Terry and her son spoke about how to discourage the monster from returning. Her son, ardent in his belief that the monster was real, decided that they should "arm" themselves against it. He drew pictures of the monster, which she helped him color in. Over the pictures, they drew the universal symbol for "Not Allowed" (a circle with a line through it), then made labels for spray bottles. Together, they concocted a ghastly mixture of liquids, then filled several atomizers with their "Monster Repellent." She and her son deposited them strategically around the house so they would be ready to fend off the monster if it reappeared, which it did not.

Whether your child awakens abruptly screaming inconsolably or looks for you in the morning still hurting from a difficult dream, you are his or her first ally. Your immediate reaction may be similar to the one you would have in a waking situation in which your child is threatened or hurt. The impulse to protect a child from a psychic danger is the same as the impulse to protect a child from a material danger. This impulse puts you, right away, on your child's side, where you are needed.

As a dreamtime ally, you cannot necessarily "fix" the situation. You can, however, listen attentively and refrain from dismissing your child's dream experience, no matter how much you might be tempted to say, "It was just a dream." You can also offer to help, as Terry did, to come up with or implement whatever rectifying scheme your child thinks up.

Sorting Out Bad Dreams and Nightmares

There is a gradation between bad dreams and nightmares. For a three-year-old, a dream in which a friend takes away a toy, or his or her parents are lost, is a bad dream. At five, the child may awaken troubled because robbers intruded or sad because a friend got hurt in a dream. Something bad happens that leaves the child upset, sad, or unsettled.

Bad dreams reflect the child's vulnerability. A child is vulnerable not only because he or she is a child, vulnerability is inherent to the human condition. To that extent, bad dreams are unavoidable. In fact, they can communicate precious information pointing to areas in which your child is vulnerable.

A nightmare has greater intensity than a bad dream. It arouses feelings of powerful, inescapable fear, horror, and distress. A nightmare—a *mare of the night*—formerly referred to a demon or evil spirit believed to plague sleeping people. In fables and legends, horses are often clairvoyant. Carl Jung noted that they represent the magic side of humans, our intuition. Also, symbolically, the horse is a guide to the underworld. Thus, the mare of the night opens one's eyes to the other side of reality and may guide one to the dark side of one's nature. Even though nightmares seem terrible, a state of emergency, they can also bring new vitality.

Like any other dream, a nightmare can provide you with important insights. Its intensity points to a condition that a child dreamer experiences as deeply threatening to his or her ego. The child may dream of falling and literally fall off the bed, of suffocating in dream smoke, or shrinking to miniature size like Alice in Wonderland. Or a monster, too large and fierce to be overcome, may appear next to the child's bed, as in Terry's son's nightmare. Remember, however, that the Senoi congratulated their children when they had a nightmare, because a nightmare is usually a sign that the child is ready to grow.

Bad dreams are more likely to portray characters from ordinary life, often recognizable and familiar (friends, schoolmates, teachers, or relatives), but sometimes unknown (thief or bad guy). Bad dreams point to a content that is closer to the dreamer's consciousness. By contrast, the images, feelings, and sensations in a nightmare stand out as *numinous,* that is, imbued with an inner power that points beyond the ordinary. The characters of nightmares are often other than human, such as creatures or animals. Nightmares come from deeper layers of the unconscious.

If a bad dream can grow to a nightmare, a nightmare can revert to a bad dream as it progresses toward a resolution. A powerful monster, for instance, may break down into small monsters in later dreams and eventually give way to a life-size challenge, as a child works his or her way through a nightmare.[1] When it comes to daily dreams, you will find that there is an infinite gradation from the worst nightmare to the most mundane bad dream.

Nightmare Triggers

Asking why children have nightmares is akin to asking a question about human nature itself. Instead of asking why, consider the most common triggers for nightmares: a child's inability to account for ordinary events in the surrounding world, a child's feelings about events of emotional significance to him or her, and a child's passing from one stage to the next with the changes and new challenges that times of transitions entail. Physical factors and situations of violence, abuse, and trauma can also trigger nightmares.

Children's Reactions to Ordinary Events in Their Surroundings

Children react to events in their surroundings that they neither understand nor control. These events play a role in some of their fears and nightmares. Here is an example. Young Tammy was approximately eighteen months old when she began repetitively awaking in the early morning, distraught and crying as she plodded into her parent's room. The recurring nightmare of a "truck hurt Tammy" was always the same. She was consoled only after she was reassured that no truck would get her and that she was perfectly safe at this time. Tammy's parents questioned each other and their nanny as to the origin of this dream, but no obvious interaction between Tammy and a truck had occurred. The scenario repeated itself many times over a period of approximately one month. Then one morning, just after she had arrived in her parents' room, Tammy's dad heard the faint sound of the early morning trash truck as it drove down their quiet street. He pointed this out to Tammy and she acknowledged that this was the truck that hurt her in her dreams. After this awareness and some continued reassurance, she stopped having the dream.

Disturbing sounds from sirens, airplanes, and household machines, or characters in costume, such as a clown at the fair or even soldiers in uniform, can induce fear in young children and trigger nightmares, like the trash truck did for Tammy. Providing reassurance to the child comes first. Providing information on the object of the child's fear can also help dispel the fear. Books on the object of a child's fear, a visit to the fire station, or a neighbor in the army can contribute to easing a child's fear and to relieving a child's nightmare.

Feelings about Events of Emotional Significance for the Child

Most bad dreams and nightmares are triggered by awake-time events with emotional significance for the dreamer. Feeling responses of pain, fear, anger, worry, and guilt to these events are the fuel for a child's bad dreams and nightmares. The events that take on an emotional significance for the child may seem benign to an outside observer or even go unnoticed. Yet they have registered on the child's emotional radar. In the dream, the child feels out of control. The child runs for his or her life. The child feels distressed, overwhelmed, or is under attack, as six-year-old Katherine (6:11) was in this nightmare:

> One time I was outside—this is a nightmare—I was outside. I wanted to catch a bird. It was a bird that was all black, you know, let's say a raven—it was a raven. And me, I wanted to catch the raven, to take it into my hands, to pet it. He got scared and he started to fly up high like this, not fast. Well, I didn't catch it. I did not succeed because it went too high. After that I went back real fast into the garage. And then there was a dark hand, which went like this—I did not see it—and it went from one point in the garage, high up and all the way down to the floor. I was seeing that. It meant to say, "That's what it is, eh? Ah! Ah! That's the hand that caught me and hurt me."

I go tell my mother twice what happened and I cry. I told her that the hand had caught me and that it had made me fall and all the rest. After that, my mom, she consoles me.

Katherine gives the key to the dream as she spontaneously makes the hand speak. The dark hand embodies the bird's voice and it threatens Katherine for catching it and hurting it. The hand's words suggest Katherine's guilt for trying to catch the bird mixed with the fear of having hurt the bird. Erik Erikson defined the psychosocial dilemma of preschoolers as "initiative versus guilt." It is not uncommon among children three to six and a half years old to have a dream in which their initiative turns to nightmare, as it did for Katherine. Luckily, Katherine had the comfort of a consoling mother "ally" at the end of her nightmare.

Strategies for gaining insight into a child's dreams are explored in chapter 8.

Times of Transition

At times of transition, between the ages of five and seven and again in adolescence, children typically have more vivid dreams, including nightmares. As they leave a place of security and launch toward the unknown, they may experience anxiety that temporarily affects the contents of their dreams. Times of passage bring about new levels of consciousness, capacities for awareness, and also sensitivities. For Timar, who came from Eastern Europe to the United States at the age of five, the transition from age five to seven was intensified by its coinciding with a transition between two worlds, two cultures, and two languages. It was a trying time for everyone in his family, and especially for his mother who had left a good position as a high school teacher to follow her husband. Timar began school not knowing a word of English. Being in an environment in which he was unable to communicate with his peers made his school experience a dreadful one. He would wake up in the middle of the night crying and screaming with nightmares. At fourteen, he looked back on those childhood years and remembered his most typical nightmares over a span of several years. He wrote:

> My typical bad dream was a nasty-looking thug coming after my nearly frightened-to-death parents with a knife, while I was in a third-person view. Eventually, my parents were slaughtered (which I never witnessed). Then everything would be quiet. Eventually, I would become the victim and I would be chased. The worst part is when I would start to run. Somehow I was always in a moon-walk style type of run. So whenever I would supposedly run, I would go two times slower than the "thing" chasing me. You would think that I was scared of the knife the pursuer had. Nope. I was scared of him tickling me to death. Yeah, it's weird, but to me, there is nothing worse than being tickled to a point where you can't breathe. So, every so often, there would be an alternate ending to my interval of pain. Such as drowning (this is interconnected with not being able to breathe), falling off of a building, or being eaten alive by flesh-devouring spiders.

Whereas we can immediately relate to parents worrying about their children's safety, we can easily miss that children worry about their parents too. Timar's dream of his parents under the threat of the nasty-looking thug reflects his fear for his parents as well as for himself in his new world. Timar told me that he also had "great, great dreams" during that era, dreams of being in a lot of sunlight in front of his house with the warm feeling of being loved. Timar struggled with his nightmares on his own, and he remembers his nightmares tapering off around age ten.

In the long run, cultivating a relationship with the fullness of one's dream life can help limit and even prevent nightmares. Incorporating dream journaling into your household makes children familiar with the world of dreams and gives them the opportunity to develop dreaming skills. When you make room for your child's dreams on a daily basis, it also gives you the opportunity to play your role as an ally when nightmares strike.

Physical Discomfort

There may also be physical factors to a child's nightmares. These should not be overlooked. The view that eating before going to sleep can cause nightmares is no longer in favor. Nevertheless, it is true that physical factors—bodily discomfort, heat, sickness, fever—can adversely affect the contents of dreams and the quality of dreaming.[2] When your child suffers from nightmares, give consideration to possible physical factors. Making sure that your child has comfortable sleeping conditions is a protection against bad dreams and nightmares.

Situations of Abuse, Violence, and Trauma

In situations of abuse, violence, and trauma, nightmares may not resolve themselves and the child then requires professional help. Nevertheless, you as a loving parent can still function as the child's ally.

Night Terrors

Night terrors are a sleep disorder that besieges some young people. These night terrors confront a family in a most troubling way. Night terrors take place at the beginning of the night. In contrast to bad dreams and nightmares, which occur during REM sleep, night terrors occur during non-REM sleep. Non-REM phases of sleep are longer at the beginning of the night and shorter as the night progresses. This explains why night terrors occur in the first half of the night.

In the grip of a night terror, a sleeper is in a kind of altered state, soaked in sweat, very agitated and breathless, with a rapidly beating heart. He or she may flail about, scream, cry, whimper, or mutter incoherently. Worst of all, night terrors render the child unresponsive. Or the child may reject parents' attempts to soothe. Just as bizarre, night terrors rarely stay within conscious reach, either at the time of the night terrors or in the morning. Only infrequently is a dream narrative associated with an episode of night terrors remembered or recounted. Sleepwalking (somnambulism), sleep talking (somniloquy), and bed-wetting (enuresis) also typically take place during non-REM sleep in the first half of the night.

If your child suffers from night terrors, the best medicine is your presence and calming voice. Restraining your child or forcing him or her out of the stupor is not recommended. Better a soothing touch. It often takes more than a few minutes for the "terrors" to run their course.

Nightmares Are but a Fragment of the Child's Dream World

In 1905, a New York newspaper, the *Herald,* began publishing Winsor McCay's comic strip, *Little Nemo in Slumberland.* A princess calls to Little Nemo every night from dreamland. In his attempt to find the princess, Little Nemo embarks on a journey through the land of dreams. But on the way, his adventure always turns to nightmare, and he never reaches his destination. Instead, Nemo wakes up in terror or falls off his bed.[3]

The publication of *Little Nemo in Slumberland* at the beginning of the twentieth century was part of a new-found interest in dreams. Although a masterpiece of poetry and invention, McCay's comic strip reflected the prevailing view that children's dreams were a source of nightmares. Since early twentieth-century families paid little attention to dreams, except for nightmares, this perspective was not surprising. Little was known then about children's dreams. The first research on children's dreams from the late 1910s to the late 1960s supported the same widespread view of children's dreams as a repository of bad dreams and nightmares.[4] It took several decades for this view to be challenged and for interest in children's dreams to grow to its present vitality.

In the late 1960s and early 1970s, laboratory studies on the content of children's dreams finally challenged the assumption that children's dreams are mostly nightmares.

Researcher David Foulkes studied the content of the
dreams of children sleeping in a dream laboratory. Three
to four times a night when they were in REM sleep, when
dream activity is at its highest, the children were awakened and their dreams were recorded. Foulkes found that
the content of children's dreams tended to reflect daily
activities rather than featuring beasts, ghosts, or other bad
types. Foulkes further showed that the dreams spontaneously reported by children represent only a small percentage of the whole of their dreams.[5,6]

Over the years, whenever I have mentioned my work
with children's dreams, many adults have hastened to
share their childhood dreams with me. Their memories of
those long-ago times were still vivid. Rare were those who
remembered beautiful or luminous dreams from their
childhood. The dreams they remembered were usually
laden with fear. And whenever I interviewed children,
they too had scary dreams to tell, dreams involving
ghosts, monsters, and biting crocodiles. Adults and children alike remember the dreams whose images and emotional content made a strong impression on them. Those
are likely to include nightmares.

Although it is true that some research indicates a
higher incidence of nightmares in children, most children's dreams are not nightmares. Dreamguiding gives
parents a firsthand perspective on the content of children's dreams. As you begin recording your child's
dreams on a daily basis, you will see for yourself that
most dreams are not fraught with danger, that nightmares
are only a limited part of a child's overall dream life. Better and even *splendid* dreams put a smattering of nightmares in perspective. When you and your child talk about

dreams daily, you will both notice that bad dreams are only a small part of the dream mosaic, and you will discover that they play an important part in personal growth.

Children's Most Typical Nightmare Themes

Each child's bad dream or nightmare is distinctive and addresses the dreamer's unique situation. Yet common themes pervade children's bad dreams and nightmares all over the world. Before anything else, my purpose here is to map the territory of children's most typical nightmares. How you can learn from and stimulate your child's creative ways of coping with bad dreams and nightmares is the focus of chapter 7.

A Dreadful Encounter: Being Chased, Bitten, Eaten Up

An encounter with a dreadful and threatening character is by far the most common nightmare in children's dreams. This dream encounter may take place in the child's bedroom or the child's house. Or the child goes on a dream adventure and has a dreadful encounter along the way. The encounter may be with a creature—a monster, a witch—or with an animal. This animal may be warm-blooded—a wolf, a tiger, a whale, a bird, an elephant; or it may be cold-blooded—a snake, a crocodile, a lizard. It can also be an insect—a spider, a bee, a caterpillar. The dreadful encounter may also be with a human—a robber, a mean king or queen; or sometimes with an object—a robot, an arrow, an ice-cream machine.

The child may only see the dreadful character and the sight of it is enough to awaken the child's terror. Or the dream character chases, bites, or threatens to eat the child. These dreams usually convey a powerful energy and this is why they are significant and memorable. "I had a scary dream," says four-year-old Madeleine:

> I went under my covers because I was afraid there was a monster coming. It looked like a T. Rex. It was trying to look through the window. It went through the glass and left a hole.

The dreadful encounter may be with a group of creatures, as it was for Hans (9:6) when he was chased by a horde of little people in his dream. The little guys were "yellow," he later told me. They "moved all together" as if they were one unit:

> There were little people with knives. I was hearing something in my bed upstairs. I came downstairs into the kitchen to see if there was something. It was coming from the basement. I went down to the basement. Then I saw all the little guys. There was a big cauldron and a skeleton in it. ("I was pretty much going nuts," joked Hans, coming out of the dream for a moment and looking at himself from an onlooker's perspective. Then he went on with the dream.) The large cauldron was hanging from the ceiling. They were running after me. There's a door in the basement. I quickly unlocked it and ran out. I didn't know where they were. I couldn't see them, but I could hear them. I checked into the barn. They were there. They seemed like they were trying to look for me. Then they saw me. I ran back to the basement and locked the door . . . They came in. They were lowering the cauldron. But before I fell into the cauldron, I woke up.

Hans associated the little guys of his dream with the characters in a book he had read. He specified, however, that the characters in his dream were different in shape and in the noises they made.

Feeling threatened, pursued, pressured, bombarded, attacked, hurt, robbed, tricked, or violated at one's boundaries in awake-time life may trigger a dreadful dream encounter. It is important to keep in mind, however, that dreams can always be read at more than one level, taking into account also the dreamer's age and circumstances.

Falling, Drowning

From the age of four on, Luke, now thirty-two, was cursed with nightmares of falling. Plummeting downward, he would wake up terrified just before hitting the ground.

"Where were you falling from?" I asked Luke.

Seeming a bit surprised by the question, as if he had never considered it, he responded, "I don't know." He confided that he still had falling dreams, but without the fear he knew as a kid.

The impulse to avoid stumbling and falling is a natural one. And, if falling, the impulse to resist the fall is a common one too.

"Did you resist when you had falling dreams?" I asked Luke.

"I did resist," he laughed, pushing his open hands into the air as if to stop himself from an imaginary fall.

In their dreams, children may fall off a building or a loft and occasionally out of an airplane. They may fall into water (waterfall, pool, river) or a pit. They may fall by accident, be pushed by a natural force like the wind, or be provoked into falling by someone who startled them when they were on the edge of a high place. In my research, I found that boys report falling dreams more frequently than girls do.

Depending on the context of the dream and the age of the dreamer, falling in a dream can be an image for failing, falling from grace, losing one's footing, losing ground, going downward, or the fear of it. Carl Jung held that, for adults, falling can be an effort of the unconscious to compensate for being "too high and mighty," or too puffed up. By contrast, the Senoi hold that falling in a dream is an invitation to meet the spirit world, and that falling can turn into flying.

Falling dreams are an opportunity to learn how to navigate dream space. In their dreams, older children show signs of learning these skills. If falling from a height toward the ground is one downward movement, sinking to the bottom of a body of water through drowning is another one. Drowning can be followed by surfacing.

A Loss: Being Lost, Losing One's Belongings, Losing a Baby

There are three typical forms in children's dreams of loss: the child is lost, the child loses his or her belongings, and the child loses a baby. The child dreams of being lost, or of losing his or her parents; for instance, losing sight of parents in a public setting. Parents are the most central and precious people in the life of a young child. Being separated from parents in a dream can be distressing to a child. Such a dream resonates immediately with a parent.

In a dream, losing something dear to one's heart, such as jewelry, a favorite article of clothing, a toy, or a pet, may be a reflection of an emotional loss in awake-time life. If one's possessions are stolen, hurt, destroyed, or misplaced in a dream, it registers as a loss of identity or soul, as with Joan (5:10) and her brand-new sandals:

> Once I had new sandals. I went to a movie, and during the movie, everybody took off their sandals, so I did it too. There was a man who came and he took my sandals and he threw them in the trash. And I lost them. My dad thought that it wasn't my real sandals. He thought it was someone else's sandals. I yelled in my dreams that I had lost my shoes.

And although they are too young to have children of their own, children can dream of losing a baby. The baby is dropped or falls. A child, a precious being, is also an image for the soul and for wholeness. In eight-year-old Eva's dream, the baby is not hers, but one dear to her:

> We were in a boat. We started going. The lady at the docks said, "You should be safe." Suddenly our whole boat went on its side. We finally got the boat back. I looked to the side. Trudy's baby was sinking. I ran to the side of the boat. "Please pull me up," said the baby. I pulled it up and carried it to Trudy and Roger. I gave Trudy THE BABY and walked AWAY to my seat! We turned on the boat's engine and left about an hour later. I heard a little splash. The baby had fallen into the water.

As the party begins its journey, the boat turns on its side. But only after the boat is upright again does Eva realize what has occurred: The baby has fallen into the water.

In the fairy tale of the handless maiden, the heroine drops her twin babies in the water. It is when she reaches out to fetch her babies from the water that her hands miraculously grow back and she is healed, whole again. In the dream, the baby calls to Eva as if Eva were the one connected to the baby. She pulls the baby out and brings it to the parents. Balance seems to be restored. Yet, as soon as the boat is on its way again, she hears a splash and, for the second time, the baby has fallen. The dream ends with the baby at large.

Children of all ages experience grief through dreams of loss.

Misfortune: Injury, Illnesses, Death

Children's bad dreams and nightmares include dreams portraying misfortunes such as injury, illness, and death. Misfortunes may befall the dreamer, or the dreamer's parents, friends, or pets, or an unknown character. In Helen's (6:2) dream, it is a child who is the victim of injury:

> I dreamt that we were at the restaurant and there was a robber who came. He had a small box and there were arms in it. It was the arms of a child.

Helen drew the mother and her child with cut-off arms. Having one's arms or hands cut off is a theme also found in fairy tales, as in the fairy tale of the handless maiden just mentioned. It may be an image for powerlessness, for losing the ability to do.

Illnesses and death are often closely associated, one leading to the other. Sometimes it is the child's whole family that is threatened. In Jude's (5:3) dream, there is "sickness stuff" on his shoes, as well as on those of his parents and sibling. To prevent his death and the death of his family, he wipes off his shoes and everyone else's. Children are attuned to their parents and affected by instability in their world. Bobbie (6:3) dreamt that her dad had died from a heart attack from smoking. (Soon after, her father quit smoking.) A week after five-year-old Karina's dad had a heart attack in the middle of the night, she dreamt that he had died. Although her parents had kept her from the family trauma by not telling her about the heart attack, unbeknownst to them she had registered the trauma, and participated in it emotionally through her dream.

Death dreams may point to an emotional death rather than a physical one, as in the case of a separation. The grief associated with the separation is felt like a death. References to death can also appear in children's dreams at times of transition from one stage to the next. Hans dreamt that his whole family was exterminated and that only he survived:

> It was in a large forest. There was like a hole full of sand. There were people I knew who lived in there. We lived in tipis. My family was separated in two. We had two tipis for our family. There were ghosts sometimes—monster-ghosts. They could become ghosts or not stay ghosts. They had harpoons for hunting. A Chief of the Territory said that in the old days, in this place, it once happened that they had been chased away by these ghosts. The others did not believe him. They thought that it was only a legend, but it was true, and it happened. Almost everyone got chased away, except for a couple of people. It was my family. Except

that my sister was dead. Then my mother died and my brother. Only my father and I were left. . . . My father died. I was the only one left; it sucked. They [monster-ghosts] did not come back. I lived until I died at the end of my life.

"It was like a village," Hans added. "I lived till the end of my life—let's say when I was a hundred. The others were exterminated."

Sooner or later, children grow out of their family to find their way into the world on their own. Hans's dream suggests a lad's intimation of his life beyond the close circle of his family and community. The dream captures a child's sense of his mortality.

Vehicular Accidents

Episodes of being the victim of a car, train, or bike accident are common misfortune-dream themes. Here is Annie's (6:1) dream:

> I had a nightmare. It's that my dad got out of the car. He was going to buy French fries. It took a long time. So we played with the steering wheel. [She imitates moving the steering wheel back and forth.] Then there was a big hill and we rolled down the hill. The car caught on fire. And we were dead. I thought that it was for real. I woke up. It was the morning and it was not for real.

As in Katherine's dream at the beginning of the chapter, the kids' initiative (in this case, playing with the steering wheel) turns to nightmare. Vehicular accidents may indicate an occurrence that derails the journey or the movement forward, or perhaps a loss of control or organization in the child's sense of self.

Natural or Human-Made Catastrophes

Children also contend with the power of natural forces, dreaming of tidal waves, earthquakes, avalanches, thunderstorms, and fires. Lucie (5:10) dreamed that her friends' house caught on fire:

> Stan and Ingrid's house caught on fire. Stan put a screw with a little bit of cotton ball in his elbow. There was a hole so it could fit in. Ingrid was scared. She was running away. I woke up and went to sleep in my mom's bed because I was afraid.

Eight-year-old Eva dreamed that a huge wave swept over her:

> I walked out onto the end of the dock. "See," I said, "I can do it." All of a sudden, S., S., and H. called out, "Watch out!" A huge wave swept over me and splashed me with water. I jumped to the other side, crying.

In these dreams, children come into contact with forces larger than themselves. Children also dream of human-made catastrophes such as wars.

Children's Recurring Nightmares

That children have bad dreams and nightmares is to be expected. A recurring nightmare, on the other hand, is like a wound never attended to or a problem never dealt with. Whereas we would never think of leaving a child with an unattended bodily wound, we may ignore a recurring nightmare, dismissing it as unimportant, childish, or "just a dream." If a child has persistent dreams of being hurt, being wounded, or drowning, parents should not hesitate to seek professional help.

First Aid for Bad Dreams and Nightmares

Let us say that a bad dream awakens your child in the middle of the night, and he cries out. Responding to the audible discomfort, you go to your child's room. He or she may still be caught in the dream and only half awake. A gentle touch on the arm helps your child reenter the body. At this point, you can listen to whatever your child can say about the dream. Recounting the dream engages your son or daughter and relieves the paralyzing effect generated by the fear of the dream. Having a loving witness also helps diffuse the sense of aloneness. Once you grasp the main thrust of what happened, you can help the child back to sleep, leaving a door open to revisiting the dream the next day: "Let's talk about it tomorrow morning." Lying next to your child for a short while is often the most efficient way of helping him or her retrieve a restful sleep. In the morning, dream journaling awaits.

Your young child's nightmares may be so real to him or her as to warrant extra measures: caulking the cracks in the wall through which the trolls are coming, closing the closet that seems inhabited, or securing the area under the bed where crocodiles are hiding. Joining your child's magical thinking is a productive way of empowering your child while appealing to his or her imagination. "How could you seal the cracks in the wall so the trolls don't come back?" you might ask. Children come up with surprising solutions sometimes. Folk beliefs also appeal to a child's imagination. There is a folk belief that open closets attract ghosts, for example. "How about closing the door of the closet so the monster cannot come in?" Or "What could you do so the crocodile won't come under your bed anymore?" These measures help ground troubled children. They refocus their attention and actively engage them in creating solutions. These are first-aid measures.

Once the traumatic moment is passed, you may find yourself asking the same sorts of questions that you ponder when your family has upheavals in the daytime: Is my child okay? Why is my child having this dream? What does the dream mean, and what can I do? Often your reflections on what might be going on in the child's life will point to a reason for the dream. Finding time to talk about the dream with your child in the morning, however, leaves the way open for the child to find *his or her own response* to the dream and to begin learning the art of dreaming.

CHAPTER SEVEN

GUIDING YOUR CHILD
THROUGH DREAM CHALLENGES

No one wants a child to be afraid or sorrowful, yet it is important to recognize that a child's nightmares can also grace his or her life. Just as waking life calls your child to grow in strength, courage, and love, so do your child's dreams. A dream adventure tests a child, forces confrontations with age-old obstacles in the dream world. After emerging victorious from a dream struggle, a child can enter a new phase with fresh confidence. Even bad dreams are good when viewed thus, because they build a stronger foundation and deepen the child's experience.

Having certain dreaming skills can help a child reach the other, more positive and resolved side of a nightmare. Some people go through their entire lives without learning these skills. Your child can cultivate them with your guidance. With practice, and with you as a loving guide, your child will develop increasing ease and adeptness.

And the skills a child develops as a dreamer carry over into the child's waking life.

Preparing for Dreamguiding

Before you do or say anything, there is work for you to do as a parent. You must first notice the resources in your child's dream strategies and become aware of benevolent allies on your child's dream path.

Noticing Resourceful Strategies in Your Child's Dreams

Young children, although not yet equipped to understand the meaning of dreams, readily relate to and describe their *behavior* within a dream. By behavior, I mean how a child acts in relationship to people, places, and events in a dream. Behavior is what he or she does. "I hid," "I fought," "I flew," and "I shouted" are a few examples.

In the following dream, Blair (4:4) describes her behavior as hiding, talking to the fish, and holding it in her hand:

> I had a dream and the fish was pretty and it went in and out of the fish tank. It was a big fish. I was hiding 'cause I was scared. I think it was in the book area. I said, "Fish don't bite me." The fish wouldn't understand. It scared me. Some were little and some were big. That one was so pretty to me. And the fish, it came near me. I put it in my hands. It didn't hurt the fish.

Enthralled by the beautiful fish that moves in and out of the fish tank, Blair is also scared by it. In the end, the fish comes near her and she befriends it.

Although paying attention to a child's dream behavior is worth doing with any type of dream, doing so with dreams in which a child is challenged to find a way through a difficult situation is most crucial. The behavior points the way to the child's *dream strategy*. Perhaps the child is running away from a tiger. Perhaps the child tricks a pursuer with a dummy. Perhaps he or she throws stones at a feared crocodile, lays a trap for a witch, or negotiates with a villain.

Strategies are key because they represent the willingness and ingenuity to respond to challenges. Oliver (4:9), who dreamt of witches, remembered his strategy as follows:

> I was in a swimming pool and I tried to squirt her, but my squirt gun sank. I tried to shoot the witch down with my squirt gun. I was in a hot tub. It was scary there.

In looking for strategies, you may at first notice only the most spectacular ones, when the child fights actively. It pays to look for the more subtle strategies as well, however, such as the child pretending to be dead to avoid being detected, cleaning the house to eliminate the witch's poison, or sending for help after being bitten. Such coping strategies seed the development of a child's dreaming skills.

By giving attention to your child's dream strategies, you will begin to discern and appreciate your child's resourcefulness as a dreamer. When considering a child's dream strategy, take into account the threat as well as the child's personality and development. Confrontation is not always the most advisable response. Fleeing can be a wise course when contending with too ominous a force. Jess (5:2) fled from a dream bear with daggered teeth:

> The bear was after me. And he was going so fast and I was right in front of his mouth and his teeth were like daggers. And he was running and I was flying

really close to the ground, close enough to run, but I decided not to because I didn't want to break the speed.

When your child is disempowered, hurt, or taken over by a dream creature, he or she may not have any obvious strategy available, except to wake up. This is fine. An incubation period is sometimes needed for a child's energy to rebound. With time and in later dreams, the child may summon the necessary strength to respond more powerfully and adroitly to a bad dream. Trust that your child will find the resources at his or her own perfect pace. Dreams are a training field, just as life is. Learning through dreaming is a process that occurs gradually.

How a child uses strategies in dreams can mirror how she or he copes with waking life's challenges. Concentrating on your child's strategies has the added benefit of helping you experience the dreams closer to the way your child does. And you make room for your child to tap into inner powers to meet the challenges and opportunities that his or her dreams present.

Becoming Aware of Benevolent Allies on Your Child's Path

Children are seldom alone in their dream worlds. Dream strategies occur in a setting with people and events. Your child's strategies to elude dangers may include receiving help from an ally. Allies may be strangers, friends, or family. They may be cultural heroes and institutional authorities such as firefighters, police, and trash collectors. There may be helpful dream animals too. In the dreamworld, as in daytime, a child will never have too broad a network of companions and friendly allies.

Adults or peers of both genders appear as dream allies. An adult ally is more likely than a peer ally to solve the problem for the child in the dream. Parents and grandparents are favorite allies against adversity. Sophie's (6:3) mom delivers her from the bad guy in the following example:

> This bad guy came along and got me in this yellow sack, and then got me in the arm. And mommy was in the car, so she got me out of his arms. And mommy kicked the bad guy over and jumped on him. And then she went inside the house and called 911. And then the police came.

In another example, Michael's grandfather rescued him from a swimming pool into which he fell in a dream. In the dream of five-year-old Françoise, it is Spider-Man who does away with the scary fox. Children can also receive help from an unknown dream character, a dream being or creature, such as the good witch in Nick's (4:10) dream:

> Mom was in this place and I was in there too. There were lots of witches and there were about two girls that I saw in the park. And then Mom disappears, and I was calling for her, but she wasn't there. I was calling, and one witch smiled at me, and said hi to me and I said hi back. And then she said, "I'll give you some help," and I was gonna say, "With your magic, can you please get my mommy back?"

Your child can ask for help in dreams when she or he is facing difficulties. When a child trusts in a dream ally for help, the dreamworld often responds favorably.

A peer ally tends to fight side by side with the child, both actively engaging in the dream's resolution.[1] A child's best friend sometimes appears as the child's companion in a dream, or as the child's ally against adversity.

Even when your child travels alone through part of his or her dream journey, there might be other "redeeming" features in the dream: a small cottage with a dog and a family in the forest where your child is lost or a board floating in the water where he falls. When all seems lost, assistance can come in the most unexpected way. Like allies, these redeeming features can bring about a turn of events. Look for redeeming features and benevolent allies in your child's dreams. They light your child's path.

Noting your child's strategies, allies, and resourcefulness inculcates a receptive spirit in you. It prepares you for dreamguiding.

Dreamguiding

Mostly children learn of the rich benefit of dreams on their own. As a dreamguider, you watch, appreciate, give a tip here, ask a question there, stand by, and reap the harvest of deeper family bonds.

Cultivating a Graceful Approach to Your Child's Dreams

The spirit with which you receive your child's dream can inspire your child's feeling for dreaming and your child's development as a dreamer. Curiosity, encouragement, respect, and love are all vital. Management is not. Prying is not. Your emotional engagement is what is important. Something as simple as taking delight in your child's dream counts. Your child will feel the open quality of your heart, even if it is only through a light tone of voice, a gracious smile, or a small comment.

When your child reports a dream, thank your child. Saying "Thank you for telling me your dream" communicates appreciation. It is also a way of recognizing your child as a dreamer and of communing with him or her through the dream. An expression of gratitude is often all that your child needs to move on and go his or her way.

Encouragement and praise embolden and lift a child's spirit, but only on the condition that they are genuine and related to events that feel true to the child. When a child dreamer encounters a scary dream creature, the bravery with which he or she tries to overcome the creature is touching, regardless of the outcome. A parent's heart goes out to the child. "Do you know what I like about your dream?" the mother or father might ask. "It is that you really tried to solve the situation you were in. Someday you will succeed." Or "Wow! You were strong when you stood up to the robber who tried to steal your car!" When your child reports that he or she received some benevolent assistance, from an animal, person, or some uncanny circumstance, you might comment, "How smart you were to know that could be helpful!" or "Wasn't that lucky!"

When you tailor your comments to what your child tells you, you support your child's learning without robbing your child of ownership of the dream.

Fostering Dreaming through to a Point of Resolution

In the West, child and adult dreamers alike do not usually know, unless they are taught, that continuing a dream is an option. This act of continuing a dream through to a point of resolution is one of the most important skills a child can develop. With practice, a child's awareness within the dream state sharpens. The child's ability to dream longer and to bring more consciousness to the dream state increases, furthering opportunities to make choices while in the dream. Sustaining focus while dreaming, a child dreamer may try to extend a good dream or, if he or she is bold, hang in there with a bad dream to solve a troubling situation.

Instructions to children about dreaming should be rare, judicious, and called forth by their need for guidance. If your child remains upset after telling a dream, invite your child to "continue the dream and see how it develops." Of course, continuing to dream is simpler right after the dream occurs. Young children live in the present, so resuming what they were just doing is usually easy. Your child can turn over, close his or her eyes, and continue to "dream," using imagination.

When continuing a dream, a child can bring in powerful allies or turn to family or institutional authorities to resolve the dream. This technique helps the child become more involved in solving a dream problem. And it often leads to a less troubling ending of the dream.

Inviting your child to continue the dream requires some restraint. Instead of calculated instructions, open-ended suggestions are best. A simple "Would you like to close your eyes and see what happens next in the dream?" is pure and unobtrusive. The idea is to give the child permission to return to the dream and to engage the child's initiative. In this way, you demonstrate your confidence in your child's creativity. Closed instructions such as "Try to confront the monster" might seem too scary. Plus they risk locking the child into a single way of dealing with the dreamworld—your way, not your child's way. Better to let the child continue the dream on her or his own, as you sit by, waiting to hear what is happening. Before you know it, you may find your child lying in bed, concentrating, and telling you, "I am looking at what happens next."

Soon after turning five, Linette dreamed that mean people turned her into an "ugly star."

"Did you have feet?" her mother asked.

"No."

"Did you have a face?"

"Yes."

"What did you look like?"

"I was all black and ugly."

"What do you think of closing your eyes again and seeing what happens with this dream?"

Linette agreed. The mean people put in traps, she reported, but she was able to jump over one after another because she was a star. She was looking for her father and called to him. Then she put a point of the star into her mouth, which she demonstrated later after the dream was over, by putting her finger into her mouth. That turned her back into a human.

Linette did not *need* her mother to make the dream better, but her mother's suggestion gave her permission to continue the dream. When left to her own resources, Linette not only dodged the dangers, but also resolved the conflict.

If a child needs encouragement to return to a dream, a parent can ask, "What can you or I do so you feel safe going back to this dream?" or even offer, "Would it help you if I held your hand?" or "Would it help you if you held your favorite blanket?"

Returning to a dream gives the child the opportunity to make better choices than before, to call for help if the need arises, and to experience a different outcome to the dream.[2] This invitation to "conscious dreaming" need not occur frequently. Even if parents summon a child to return to a dream only once or twice, they have planted a seed. Children learn that reentering a dream is possible. They will then do this on their own. Most important, the capacity to continue a dream to its resolution may carry over into the uninterrupted dream state.

Children quickly pick up on the idea of interacting with their dreams. Carol, a university professor friend of mine, had her five-year-old grandson Philip for the night. While he was there, she was writing to her seven-year-old nephew who was afraid to go to sleep at night because of nightmares. In her letter, she told the seven-year-old about my study on children encountering monsters in their dreams.[3] She told him that some children combat the monster, but others end up befriending it in the dream. After she finished her letter, she read it aloud to Philip. The next morning, Philip woke up saying that he dreamt of a machine. The machine transformed into a bad man, but he befriended him. At the age of five, he had immediately applied to his dream what he had learned the day before.

Many a nightmare is an unfinished dream. The ability to hold one's focus in a dream allows a child dreamer to continue dreaming until landing safely, coming to the end of an adventure, savoring a magical encounter, tasting the exhilarating feeling of swimming, singing, flying in a dream, or discovering a hidden treasure. By guiding dreaming through to a point of resolution, parents give their child the opportunity to develop as a dreamer. Continuing to dream is a concept that a child can grasp.

Modeling a Problem-Solving Attitude

Sometimes a child finds a dream enemy too powerful and threatening, and it may not feel right to invite the child to risk reencountering it by going back to the dream. A less scary, more indirect approach is to find out more about the dream enemy in a warm, cozy, and awake exchange with the child. You can explore a dream's content by asking simple questions. This helps your child appraise the dream opponent and reflect back on the dream from an alert state. Such an exploration may also set a process of resolution in motion.

Remember, however, that children do not like to be questioned in any systematic way about their dreams. When asking questions about a child's dream, stay in touch with the flow of the moment and attune to the child's interest.

Shortly before Annabelle (5:11) turned six, she woke up one morning shouting in her sleep, "Mommy! Mommy!" She was terrified because a wolf had appeared at her bedside.

As it turned out, Annabelle's father came to her room. "How big was the wolf?" he wanted to know. Still shaking, Annabelle held up her hands to show that it was a full-grown wolf. "What color?" asked her dad.

"Light brown and dark brown and some black," said Annabelle.

"Like the Siberian wolves we saw at the zoo?"

"Not like those. A little bit smaller."

"Was it a he or a she?"

Annabelle did not know but added the extra information that "it was a grownup trying to catch his or her
prey."

"Where did he or she want to bite you?"

"He didn't want to bite me," said Annabelle. "He
wanted to eat me all up."

"Gosh, if you had continued the dream, what do you
think would have happened?"

"I didn't want to continue the dream. If I had, I think
that he would have eaten me. That's why I shouted out
for Mommy."

In a gentle way, Annabelle's father directed Annabelle
to turn toward the figure of the wolf again. In addition, he
invited her to exert her intellectual curiosity about an
emotionally laden image. His bond with her made for a
safe interaction.

This, however, was a dream challenge for which
Annabelle had no available response, nor did her father.
Yet like throwing pebbles in the water, he asked questions
hoping to stir something in Annabelle's unconscious that
might ripple in later dreams.

A few days later, Annabelle had another wolf dream,
in which she encountered the wolf at the Three Little
Pigs' house. As she recounted:

> Once upon a time, we were staying with the
> Three Little Pigs for a weekend. You guys [her par-
> ents] went upstairs to read. I met the wolf in the
> house. I said, "I will show you where your food is." I
> took a little clicker and I clicked wherever I wanted.

He thought that the clicker was food. I pushed the wolf's head down where I pretended his food was. The wolf saw that there was no food. He tried to karate me, but I was best at karate-ing him. And I killed the wolf. And the little pigs sang, "Annabelle killed the wolf. Annabelle killed the wolf." And we lived happily ever after.

In this case, Annabelle evidently profited from reading "The Three Little Pigs" and from having control of the clicker. The pigs vanquished the wolf in the story and, in so doing, showed Annabelle the way. In the dream, they helped her celebrate her victory. Moreover, in her second dream, Annabelle was no longer alone. Her folks were in the background, giving her the confidence to interact safely with the wolf. It might even be that her father's interest in the first wolf dream inspired some of this confidence.

Annabelle's dream resolution was fairly typical. When children approach a territory that is loaded with fear, they often resort to a well-known pattern—a model from a story, movie, video game—to respond to the situation. Fairy tales, for instance, are replete with characters that show how to cope with dark figures. Children identify with the heroes and heroines of these stories, and model their own behavior after theirs. A pattern like the three pigs struggling with the wolf provides a structure within which the child can move, experiment, and experience a successful outcome. Victories in these settings may prepare a child for a more personal response to a dream challenge later on.

As you can appreciate from Annabelle's experience

and, no doubt, the experience of your own child, a powerful and puzzling dream can greatly stimulate the child's dream mind. As a dreamguider, you make room for this process, witnessing it, and aiding it when called to do so. You take your cues from your child and from the dream. Remember that your dreamguiding task is to be responsive to your child and to serve his or her dream process without interfering with it, getting ahead of it, or distorting it.

Trials in fairy tales often come in threes. In a similar fashion, the wolf appeared three times in Annabelle's dreams. A few weeks later, Annabelle had another dream:

> I had a bad dream. I was with Sean at Sean's house. Sean and I went to seek on a journey. We came to a castle. We entered the castle. We went down a tunnel. We heard a growl. We tried to get away. We could not get away, so we hid. Then the wolves dashed in. Then Sean jumped up and he scared all the wolves away, except one who wanted to eat me. Then I said, "Please, wolf, don't eat me," and the wolf stepped back. Then I said, "Please, dear wolf, don't eat me," and he ran away.

This was Annabelle's personal victory. Grounded within her fear, Annabelle pleaded with the wolf not to eat her. The wolf withdrew, never to come back. After she told her dad the dream, he sensed the freshness of the encounter. "I like the way you behaved in your dream," he told her. "It was brave of you to ask the wolf not to eat you. I am proud of you."

"I am proud of myself too," said Annabelle.

This is dreamguiding at its best.

Standing by as a Dreamguider for an Older Child

Often the challenging enemies of dream tests reappear, as the wolf did for Annabelle, giving an opportunity to "retest" until the dreamer has successfully met its challenge. Standing by as a dreamguider for an older child, seven and older, parents can sometimes recognize the recurrence of an image from earlier childhood. The child's growth shows in how the images and strategies that resolve dreams develop.

At the beginning of this chapter, I reported Jess's dagger-teeth bear dream. Two years later, bears returned in one of his dreams. Jess (then 7:6) was a caveman in his dream. "I found myself in a cave," he began. "I was like a caveman too and there was lots of other cavemen around in that cave." The action of the dream begins with Jess encountering two bears:

> I was going inside the cave when I saw two bears. There was another person beside me. And those two bears tried to jump on top of us. But me and this other guy helped them out to the side. Then we ran into the cave, and the bears charged at us. So we kicked them and hit them with a little hard thing that the cavemen have, hit them on the head. So we kept on doing that until they were all gone.

The bears attack as if they were guarding the entrance to the cave. Jess, with the help of his ally, another caveman, fights the bears until they are completely gone. Having succeeded in putting the bears to flight, Jess then has access to that part of the cave where the men dwell. There he has the following encounter with a girl:

> Then I went to where lots of other cavemen were in the cave, and one of the girls said, "I'll throw this necklace to you and you try to catch it." So she threw it and I got it. And then I threw it back to her, then I moved to the side. She tried to throw it back to me, but someone else got it. And she kept on throwing it to me, but other people kept on getting it.
>
> She said, "Why don't you take me to another place?"
>
> And then I said, "I can just open my eyes and the dream will be over."
>
> But she said, "No."
>
> So I found a place to go with her. And then, as I was coming back into the room, I opened my eyes.

The dream necklace is an image for a bond or tie, a link, *a connection*. The dream portrays an encounter with a soul mate, an inner image of the opposite gender. The dream points to a new developmental stage for Jess. Dreaming through to a point of resolution blossomed into lucid dreaming when Jess became aware within the dream state that he could bring the dream to an end by opening his eyes. Instead, he chose to continue dreaming in response to the girl's objection to ending the dream. Still dreaming, he found a place to go with the girl. Then coming back into the room, he opened his eyes.

The empowerment that a dreamer feels in dreams

affects the dreamer's sense of self in future dreams and in life as well. Many more encounters await the developing dreamer. These encounters will further the child dreamer's growth.

The process of recording the dreams of an older child, age eight through ten, can remain a precious interaction for both parents and child. As children mature, parents gradually relinquish their role as dreamguiders, and children take over the guide role for themselves. Thus they learn firsthand that dreams are nourishing and teaching, and that dreams will guide them.

When the recording stops, sharing dreams and talking about them with teenagers keeps the dream legacy alive and adds another dimension to family life. Your participation as a dreamguider fortifies your child's selfhood while deepening your family's bond of love.

Chapter Eight

Dream Gifts for Parenting

Attuning to Your Child's Feelings

Parents do not always know what impacts their children emotionally. As you may already be aware, any insight is more like a hunch than a clearly formulated thought, yet an insight still changes your consciousness once you receive it. Your children's dreams can deliver fresh insights into their feelings, because dreams are their unconscious means of seeking resolutions to challenges.

Imagine for a moment that you and your preschooler go trick-or-treating with other families on a warm moonlit Halloween evening. The neighborhood is lit with imaginatively handcrafted pumpkins at almost every doorstep. Several houses have elaborate decorations. Your jolly little group goes from door to door, at times passing other groups of trick-or-treaters in costumes. Your kids return from their round with an abundant harvest of candy and treats of all sorts. A perfect evening, you think to yourself. But lo and behold, your child wakes up the next morning with a nightmare. In the dream, a pirate threatened to take your child away. You remember that at one house the night before, a man dressed as a pirate greeted your group. Something triggered the dream, likely a fear or impression associated with the pirate. Without the dream, you would never have known that there was some shadow for your child on that seemingly perfect evening.

Like adults, children do not consciously register every malaise, much less report it. Experiences and changes are abundant and fleeting during childhood, particularly in these over-scheduled times. Beginning school or changing teachers from one year to the next can be anxiety-laden passages for children. Although on the surface children may seem to adapt to changes with a natural ease, underlying concern and anxiety may show through their dreams. A girl entering second grade dreamt that she had been assigned the wrong teacher and, of course, the very one she would have wished not to have. A well-behaved boy dreamt that he was expelled from school on the first day of his entering middle school for some wrongdoing unbeknownst to him.

Conflicts with friends, school pressure, under-performing, and discord or instability in the family are occasions of stress for children, which may percolate through to their dreams. Keeping pace with feelings is more and more challenging. Dreamguiding helps you stay tuned to the emotional layer of your children's life experiences: the fears, frustrations, and hurt feelings related to the events of their experiences as well as what fulfills, nurtures, and delights them. Slowing down for nighttime and then enquiring in the morning after dreamtime affords us a heartfelt means of connecting with our families.

Making Sense of Your Child's Dream

Taking the Dream at Face Value and Then Beyond

Dreams can be enigmatic. You might be at a loss when faced with your child's dream, for dreams speak in images and most of us are untutored in deciphering the meaning of symbols. Maybe you have been conditioned to believe that only a specialist can understand dreams. Yet experience teaches that dreams are a resource of human imagination for everyone to tap into, explore, grow with, be guided by, and enjoy.

Recognizing a dream's simple facts initiates the process of making sense of a dream. If a four-and-a-half-year-old wakes up in tears from dreaming that he is at Disneyland with his dad while his mom is at work and that he misses her, the child obviously is missing his mommy. Exploring the surrounding circumstances in the dream may help generate fresh points of view. What are the circumstances in the dream in which the child misses the mom? The mom is *at work*. Are the demands of the mom's work taking her away from her child? The child is at Disneyland, the land of *play,* when he misses the mom. Does the mom spend enough time playing with her child? As these questions come up, one after the other, the mom is naturally led into a process of reflection on her parenting presence with her child. This is the obvious but not the only reading of the dream.

Then, beyond the facts of the dream, a deeper layer

of making sense of the dream can open. Missing one's mom may symbolize losing touch with oneself or being estranged from oneself, as a mom can stand for a young child's center in a dream. After a long day at Disneyland, a tired child will miss the comfort of home and Mom, even if the child is with a loving daddy. Reconnecting with Mom is akin to reconnecting with oneself. (Reflexively, your child may stand for your soul in your dreams and losing your child in a dream can mean losing touch with the essential.)

A dream is new information. It reveals rather than disguises. When a dream portrays known people, such as the mother in the previous example, it is reasonable to assume at first that the dream figure refers to the real person. But it is also enlightening to consider that known people in dreams may be symbols that point to something other than themselves, like the mother standing for the child's center or mediating for the child's center. The meaning of a dream is better amplified by generating several points of view.

Carrying the Dream within Oneself

Some dreams are predominantly symbolic. At their center is a snake, a forest, water, fire, or some other dream symbol. Even with symbolic dreams, practicing taking the dream at face value is a good place for you to begin. If a monster in a dream chases your child, it is reasonable to assume that some real-life "monster" *is* chasing the child, that is, *something is dogging or pressuring* him. If your child dreams that she was lost in the forest and that she found her way home, it is reasonable to assume that the child *was* lost in the forest, that is, *she was in a state of confusion or was without a sense of direction* for a while. You can rejoice that she found her way home.

The word "symbol" comes from the Greek *symbale,* which means "to resonate." A dream resonates within the heart and soul. Carl Jung suggested carrying a dream "within oneself" as a means of gaining insight into it. This advice serves for your own dreams, your child's dreams, and anyone's dreams. When your child receives a dream that puzzles you, holding it in your consciousness as you go about your day is a way to begin making sense of it. In the midst of a conversation with a colleague, while reading a newspaper, or during a walk at the lake, elements of an answer may come to you. Carrying the dream within, you will feel its emotional charge, and your thoughts will begin to shift. Quietly into your heart, the dream will begin to speak its soft resonance.

A parent's approach to understanding a child's dreams is mostly intuitive and spontaneous. But occasionally, parents also gain insight into a child's dream from a story. Associating a dream image with a similar image from a fairy tale, a Bible story, or a work of children's literature assumes that dream images are universal symbols. Over time and across cultures, dream symbols have recurred. How a motif works and develops in a story may give you insight into how a similar motif may work and develop in your child's dreams or life. If a child dreams that a whale ate her up after she drowned in the ocean, the story of Jonah from the Bible may help throw light on the child's dream. Jonah's refusal to follow God's order, the stormy sea into which he is thrown, and his release from the whale after three nights and three days may reveal a possible outcome for the child's dream journey. Perhaps, like

Jonah, the child will emerge from the belly of the whale and be renewed.

To learn more about a particular dream symbol, a dictionary of symbols can come in handy as a tool. A good dictionary of symbols lists several points of view on a given symbol. These are the traditional thoughts and ideas that people from different cultures and times have had on the symbol. By browsing through a dictionary of symbols, you can gather information to feed your reflection on a dream and stimulate your imagination. Numerous dictionaries of symbols are available. My favorite is *A Dictionary of Symbols,* by Jean Chevalier and Alain Gheerbrant, translated from the French by John Buchanan-Brown. It is comprehensive and available in paperback.

Not all dreams reveal their secrets. But if you get a single insight from your child's dream, that is enough. If you gain a sense of direction for parenting, shift a point of view, change an attitude, or are renewed in your appreciation for your child as a result of a dream, the dream has granted its gift.

Understanding Your Child's Dream Processes

Discerning Recurring Patterns in Your Child's Dreams

Your child's dreams may seem to be uncoordinated, disparate, and without any organizing principle. Yet when we look at a child's dream journal, we find that certain themes, strategies, and patterns that were in seed form at the beginning of a child's dream life at three and four years old reappear and undergo development over time. Certain dream themes recur for years. A child dreamer's relationship with certain dream characters and dream dynamics also evolves over time.

A child's life unfolds as if in a spiral and parents can draw insights by connecting dreams or elements of dreams. Parents can sometimes recognize a challenge a child is struggling with in more than one dream. A child preparing to go on a trip away from home for the first time may have more than one dream related to the adventure on which he or she is preparing to embark. Like the spokes of a wheel, a series of dreams focused on one challenge all point toward the same center.

When a child's dream leaves you perplexed, rereading the preceding dreams in your child's dream journal may help you gain insight. Often, you will find that an earlier dream leads to the dream that puzzles you. Hugh was pursued by waves in a dream. As I flipped through the pages of his dream journal one day, I discovered that a month or so before he had had another wave dream. In that previous dream, he was out in the sea when "a big big wave came and knocked a boat over." A more peripheral motif in the first dream, the waves were at the heart of the second dream. And whereas in the first dream, Hugh was only a witness of how the big wave had knocked the boat over, in the second dream he himself was threatened by the waves and had to confront their power. It is often only in hindsight that parents discern the development of a dream motif through a small series of dreams and witness their child's progression toward resolution. Seeing a dream as part of a series puts it in context. In a similar way, when a dream causes parents to wonder, they can also watch for the next dreams. The theme may recur, revealing a development of the issue at hand.

Dreams connect over large spans of time as well. Occasionally, we can recognize dream developments over a several-year span. When she was five, Emily's family left their home in coastal California to vacation along the Saint Lawrence River. Large bodies of water such as oceans and wide rivers, with the tremendous power of their waves or flow, can be intimidating to children. Tides are another impressive phenomenon in a river this size, particularly at high tide when the water closes in on the land. When she came back from vacation, Emily dreamt that her family was in the house by the river and the tide was high. The water was coming all the way to the house. There was a little window at the level of her knees and there was a small crack at the bottom of the window. She was afraid that the water would come in.

Four years later, when her family went back to the river for summer vacation, they took Emily's best friend with them. The two girls met and played with a group of three other girls who lived there. Shortly after Emily returned home, she had the following dream:

There's this house thing. It was like a house, except that it was not like a house. One of the walls was missing. It was the wall facing the Saint Lawrence River. The waves were very big. They came all the way up over the sand, over the grass and into the house, and then out again. We played in the house and we let the waves chase us. The house was the house next door to our cabin. After a while, when the waves came up, there was this lizard kind of creature that came with it. It came with the waves and back out. One time it started chasing me all around. Somehow

it switched and I started chasing him and then somehow it went away.

The second part of the dream took place back at
Emily's home. In the dream, the three friends now live in
Emily's home neighborhood and Emily's best friend is
there too. The five of them play hide-and-seek.

Between the two dreams, Emily's world had expanded.
The fear in the first dream that the water would enter the
house was no longer there in the second dream. The opening of a small crack in the small low window was now a
whole wall missing. That wall missing was the one facing
the river. The waves were washing in and out of the house,
and the children were playing at letting the waves chase
them in the house. A lizardlike creature came and went
with the waves—chased, was chased, and went away.

At the end of the dream, the five friends reconvene in
Emily's neighborhood back home. Through the magic of
the dream and beyond time and space, two worlds—the
summer friends by the river and the world back home—
merge into one and the play with friends goes on.

A Dream Is Incubating in the Child's Soul

Not only is there continuity in a child's dream life,
but there is also a constant interplay between a child's
daily life and his or her dreams. Tommy (11:11), who
plays the violin in his school orchestra, dreamt that he
went to rehearsal, but found the room unoccupied and
the door closed:

> I was going to orchestra like I do in the morning
> and the door was closed. I was just standing there. I

remember missing the bus and being stuck there overnight at the orchestra outside, 'cause they never opened the door. Everyone was gone. And then I woke up—and I went to orchestra!

A week before he had this dream, Tommy had gone to orchestra in the morning to find, just as in his dream, that the door was closed. He waited and no one came. Eventually, he went to the main office to telephone his mom to ask her to pick him up and drive him to school. His mom did not answer when he called, but then she called him back. Fortunately, she was not far away and came to pick him up and drive him to school. His mom realized that there was no orchestra rehearsal that day. The dream captured the depth of Tommy's disarray when he found the door closed and felt unsure that his mom would be able to come soon enough for him to be able to make it to school on time. Being left alone at the door grew in the dream into the dreadful scenario of being left alone outside all night long.

Tommy immediately recognized the connection between his dream and the incident of the previous week. He was also amused that he was waking up from a dream about going to the orchestra the very morning he was going to orchestra. In fact, his having to go to orchestra that morning might very well have conjured up the memory of his previous experience and his feelings associated with it, prompting the dream. The coming together of the dream, the school incident, and his going to orchestra that morning brought a burst of laughter to Tommy and obvious relief from his disquiet.

Even though parents might be baffled or unsettled by

their children's awake-time challenges, they can trust their children's inner methods—dreams—for dealing with those challenges creatively and constructively.

Children invest their emotional energy in their friends, activities, and pets. When a child's energy, which was targeted in a given direction, suddenly has no outlet in the external world due to a momentary disruption in a friendship, not making a team, or a beloved pet dying in an accident, it goes underground, where dreams are forged. When a shadow passes over your child's heart, he or she might not have any dreams at first. During this standstill, you can watch for a dream that might be incubating in the secret of your child's soul. A dream might soon cast a fresh light for you both.

Reading Shifts in Dream Patterns

Sometimes your insight comes not from the images of a dream, but from a shift in the pattern of your child's dreams. Over time, you will become familiar with this pattern. When the dreams differ in character from those you are used to, it might simply be that the child is changing and growing into new territories. The dreams may be more vivid, the imagery more intense, revealing new levels of awakening in the child's consciousness.

Dream patterns may also shift when your child is ill. The dreams may have less vitality, color, light, or energy. They may be repetitive, with recurring images. They may also be nightmarish. Likewise, under accumulated emotional stress, the content and the fabric of a child's dreams may be affected. It may seem as if the fabric of dreams was distended and thinned out, perhaps an expression of the emotional body of the dreamer thinned out by emotional tension. Elements of being ungrounded may also show in the dream imagery.

When parents recognize from a shift in dream pattern that a child is undergoing a change or is faced with a trying time, being present to the child so he or she can move through a time of challenge with grace is the most loving thing to do. If the change perseveres and the parents grow concerned about the child's health, they should consider seeking professional help.

Dream Talk

Dream telling can blossom into a tête-à-tête between parent and child. "I wish you had a baby," announces a four-and-a-half-year-old to her mom after dreaming that the family had a baby. The dream suddenly opens an opportunity for a conversation on the topic. Or a six-year-old reflects to his dad after dreaming of having a pet that he would like to have a pet. Then he confides, "I want to be a veterinarian when I grow up." When a child discloses her or his heart's desire to a parent after a dream and the parent is receptive to the child, the moment mingles their souls.

At other times, a child's dream brings to the surface a problem the child is contending with. "I don't want to go back to day care," the child blurts out, right after telling a dream. The dream gives the parent the occasion to explore with the child what went on at day care the day before and to look with the child for solutions to the problem. Children can be better than adults at processing their dilemmas through dreaming. And sometimes a brief exchange of points of view after a dream helps put words to the felt sense of a dream.

Dream sharing becomes a way of relating to one another within a family long past childhood. Even with college kids, dream sharing can establish an instant communion that bridges distance between parents and young adults who have already left home to find their way in the world.

Dream Guidance

In their dreams, children may access a deeper knowing. This deeper knowing imparts wisdom and guides them in their waking life. Being shorter than average for his age at twelve, Jasper was contending with the demanding challenge of coping with peers who made fun of him because of his size. He had a dream:

> I dreamt that I was tall and then I made fun of one of the people who was making fun of me. They were calling me fat and big foot, because I was taller than other people. Then in the dream I was about the same size as them, so they called me nerdy. Then I was my actual size and they made fun of me—but I was used to this.

"I am pretty short for my age," reflected Jasper. "I think the reason why I had the dream is every night I wished that I was taller than them or the same size as them. This is why I was changing size in the dream. So, I realized that it didn't matter whether I was tall, short, or normal, they were making fun of me anyway. So I realized that I might as well stay the way I am 'cause I am used to it."

Jasper found confirmation for being himself through his dream.

Sometimes what a child knows in a dream does not appear to be reconcilable with reality, until a turn of events. A friend of mine called one day and told me that a cat in her neighborhood had chosen her linen closet as a nest. Soon, she expected, the cat would give birth and there would be kittens to give away. The day came when my husband, our daughter, and I took a family trip to our friend's house to see the kittens. Our friend took the time with our daughter to show her the newborns. The first kitten that caught our child's eye was the only small black female, but we learned that someone had already requested it. The other kittens were an orange tiger and a few gray tabbies. We spent time with the kittens and agreed to call the next day with our decision on which cat we would adopt. On the way home, our six-year-old confided that her favorite cat was the black one. She mused on which one of the other kittens she would choose if she absolutely had to.

The next morning she woke up with a dream:

> I had a sad dream. I had a black cat and I was all dressed in white. There was a witch and she had a white cat. She was always dressed in black. The witch killed my cat. They gave her poison to resuscitate her into a bad cat that would scratch me. The cat was red after it had taken the poison. One day it scratched me right in the middle of the face and almost scratched my eye out. Then I told the witch if you make my cat nice again, and not scratching me, I will be your friend. She did not have any friends, so she accepted.

This was not the first time, I recalled, that she had a black cat as her dream companion. She had once dreamt of waking up on her birthday and going outside to find flowers everywhere. Her dad and I were outside and we gave her a cat as a birthday gift. The cat didn't obey her, so she took it back to the store and instead got a "really sweet kitten" and "it was black."

I called my friend later that morning, as agreed, and shared the dream with her. Then I let her know that we would pick up one of the cats, most likely the orange tiger one. A couple of hours later, my friend called back, saying that, lo and behold, the black kitten was available. The woman who had reserved it, upon seeing the pictures of the kittens, had immediately fallen in love with the grey tabbies and wanted one of them. Our course was clearly laid. The black kitten could be my daughter's, making the ultimate gift of her dream a dream come true.

Catching a Glimpse of a Child's Spirit

Caught up in the pressures of daily life, hurried parents sometimes forget who their child is beneath the surface of day-to-day activity. Then, one morning, in a dream, their ten-year-old is walking with a golden retriever, her hair flowing all the way down to her waist. Or their eight-year-old is flying with his dad to the clouds to stop the rain. Or their three-year-old is rescuing a fish from sharks, to everyone's astonishment. The dream reminds them of the child's spirit. Parents suddenly see their child afresh and their appreciation for their child is renewed, often for days to come. Catching a glimpse of your child's spirit through the lens of his or her dream is one of the many unsuspected gifts a child's dreams can bring to your parenting.

Daily Renewal

Dreams spring from the waters of life. They move the dreamer to awe, fear, and dread; to grief and sadness; to love, joy, and laughter. Children wake up sometimes in tears from a dream experience, sometimes scared, sometimes bursting with a desire to have a beautiful dream come true.

Because we so love our children (and learn from them), their dreams bring daily renewal not only to them, but to us as well. Pay attention to how your child's dream can fill your day. When your child has received a beautiful dream, a feeling of peace comes upon both of you. At other times, your child's dream gives you something to contemplate and wonder about, or something to look at in yourself. At still other times, children's dreams bring a note of humor to life, and over and over again they give to us parents the gift of the unexpected and of extra connection to those we most love.

CHAPTER NINE

CALLED BY YOUR
CHILD'S DREAMS

You may often appear in your son's or daughter's dream. After all, you're one of the most familiar people in his or her young life. As characters in a child's dreams, parents do not usually predominate, but stay instead in the background. Now and then, however, a dream features a parent in enough detail that his or her traits come into sharp focus. Motivated by their love for their children, mothers and fathers can put these dream details to work to help them grow as parents. This is the next frontier of dreamguiding.

Dreamguiding is a reminder that we are not born as parents. We become parents, and we learn how to be better parents as we go along, often taught by the very people we are responsible for, our children. Parenting puts us face to face with ourselves like nothing else. Sometimes a dream mirrors the loving bond between a parent and a child. Other times, it reflects the role that a parent plays in a child's life. In dreams, as in life, parents usually protect against adversity. They console and guide. In dreams, as in life, children cast their deeds before their parents to receive recognition. Parents can also accompany a child on a dream adventure. When a dream portrays the parents' bond with a child in a positive light, parents feel in tune with their child.

Other dreams point to momentary gaps in parents' connection with a child. Even though these dreams can be troubling, they are also useful, for they reveal the child's perspective about the parental relationship. A child might dream of being in tears because Mommy or Daddy did not bestow a treat or broke a promise. Other dreams point to those moments when parents overstep their boundaries with a child. Seeing how a child demonstrates feelings about your role in his or her life may be a signal to fine-tune that relationship with your child.

Mending Your Bond with Your Child

From Mending Your Bond to Mending Your Soul

The Senoi teach that a child who is the victim of a friend's aggression in a dream should tell the friend about it in waking life and give that friend the opportunity "to repair the damage to his or her image."[1] Likewise, when a child shares a dream in which a parent hurts his or her feelings, the child is providing the parent the opportunity "to repair the damage to his or her image." The Senoi approach to mending a bond using dreams works especially well with young children, for whom dreams are so real.

If you learn that you have hurt your child's feelings in a dream, repairing your bond is your first step. When she was five, my daughter woke up one morning with the following dream:

> I dreamt that you yelled at me because I had jumped into the pool with my nightgown. And it was just a little wet. And I didn't even yell at you. I showed you that I could walk on the bottom and I jumped from the side. I don't want you to yell at me. You should never yell at me, not in a dream, not in real life.

What got my attention when I first heard the dream was the fact that I yelled at her in the dream, and I saw that she was affected by that. "I'm sorry I yelled at you in your dream," I answered. "You're right. I should never yell at you, not in a dream, not in real life."

In spite of our best intentions as parents, we sometimes hurt our children. Saying no to a child, not keeping a promise, or calling a child names can break a child's heart. Acknowledging wrongdoing has an immediate effect, however. It stops a pattern. A pattern might run like this: You yell at your child, the child feels hurt and angry so the child talks back at you, and the cycle perpetuates itself.

When genuinely felt, an apology is a gesture that infuses a relationship with grace. When we apologize to a child for a dream behavior, we also communicate to the child that we take responsibility for the behavior. It relieves the child of his or her hurt feelings. It relieves us too from the feeling of having offended our child. When we extend an act of compassion toward our child, we extend one toward ourselves at the same time. Our apology re-establishes balance and sets a child's heart free.

If mending our bond with our child after hearing a dream is the first thing to do, it is not the last. We can take one more step and use the child's dream to improve our parenting. Even though we did not participate directly in the hurt that happened in the dream, the dream has portrayed what might have been our reaction in a similar situation, at least from the perspective of the child's dream self. That child's perspective is important. Stimulated by the dream, we have the opportunity to reflect on our behavior and its impact on the child, and to bring more consciousness to our parenting.

According to Hal Edward Runkel, author of *Scream-free Parenting,* what prompts a parent's yelling behavior is anxiety. We feel so responsible for our children, he says, that we become anxiety-driven, orbiting frantically around them, and "emotionally reactive."[2] Making time and space to reflect on a dream our child has handed us prepares us to *act* instead of *react* the next time a similar situation occurs in waking life. *To act* is to respond to a situation from a place of connectedness with ourselves. It allows for a creative, fresh response to a situation. In contrast, *to react* is to respond from a pre-scripted pattern triggered by fear, anger, or anxiety.

"How bold of her to jump into the pool with her nightgown," I thought in retrospect. I also saw how focusing on the nightgown getting wet made me unavailable to her and to what she was showing me she had achieved. I felt grief. I never forgot this small dream of my daughter's. Later on, I revisited the dream and envisioned how I would have liked to play my part instead: I saw myself sitting by the side of the pool, quietly watching her, and joining her in rejoicing in her achievement. Doing so, I reconnected with her in the dream. In the years since then, I have appeared in several of her dreams. To this day, through her dreams, I still learn about myself as her parent.

Re-envisioning yourself in a dream, you can amend or revise your behavior in a way that better meets your heart's promptings as a parent, and you can complete your interaction with your child in a more satisfying way. At the same time, you are rehearsing your behavior for the next similar occasion in waking life. And in "repairing the damage to your image," you mend your soul.

Like a Magic Mirror

Not all dreams are plainspoken or easy to respond to on the spot. Some are symbolic and call for time to live with them, to consider them in more detail. Eight-year-old Joan dreamt that her dad was giving his exclusive attention to his new girlfriend. Joan's dream appears in Ann Sayre Wiseman's *Nightmare Help:*

> I am with my daddy. He's divorced. He takes me out in his boat. I fall overboard and drown. He doesn't notice because he's with his new girlfriend.[3]

The dream reveals the depth of a child's despair when a parent fails to be emotionally present to her. Joan was angry: "He's always talking to his girlfriend and forgetting about me." She drew her dream. The next time her dad came to the house to take her for the weekend, Joan showed him the drawing that she had made of her dream.

Joan's dad was likely taken by surprise and unprepared for Joan's dream. The dream revealed an uncomfortable truth. At the time, he laughed and said that she had a pretty good sense of humor. Making light of the dream by laughing and commenting on her sense of humor was a way to deflect the emotional impact of the dream. But "that weekend," Joan observed, "he didn't ignore me as much."

A child's dream can function as a parent's conscience. Although it did not bring about a full reversal, Joan's dream led to a correction in her dad's behavior. A child's dream can be more eloquent than many words. It paints an emotional reality as a child experiences it. The dream clearly indicates the direction to Joan's heart. Joan wants her dad to behave toward her in a way that lets her know he cares about her. A dream does not judge. It comes from beyond the child's conscious will. It moves the parent who hears it, if the parent is open.

In this regard, I agree with Siegel and Bulkeley that children's dreams are "truly a magic mirror":

> This is where children's dreams can be so valuable, because in their dreams, children are able to express feelings and emotions that are too difficult for them to articulate directly to their parents. The goal for parents is to learn how to listen to this indirect, but for children less intimidating, form of communication. In this way, children's dreams are truly a magic mirror, reflecting back to parents a true and honest picture of their influence on their children.[4]

In a dream-receptive household, parents are already open to receiving dreams. The children are also confident that they can share their dreams safely. When a child shares a dream with us and we do not know what to make of it at first, it remains important to acknowledge the dream to the child. We might say, to use Joan's dream as an example, "I am sorry I was not paying attention to you in your dream and I am very sorry that you fell and drowned in the dream. I would be horrified if that happened to you. It would break my heart because I love you so much. I would like to think about this dream some more. Thank you for telling me your dream." The child then knows that we have heard the dream and are willing to consider it and to take responsibility for our dream behavior.

Children's dreams are a most intimate and quiet way to learn about ourselves as parents. Welcome what your child's dreams reveal to you about yourself and honor it. Take the dream hints to reposition yourself in your relationship with your child. Mend your bond with your child. Bond mending is part of maintaining a cherished relationship on good terms. It also builds resilience into the fabric of that relationship.

Some Dreams Speak to Parents Indirectly

Some dreams do not portray the parents themselves. Yet, when parents hear these dreams, something about them may make them ponder an attitude or behavior. Eleven-year-old Tim dreamt about a robot chasing him. Tim's dream is also reported in *Nightmare Help:*

> I dreamed that a monster robot was chasing me all over the house with alarm signals screaming and lights flashing. I was so scared I started to scream. My own noise woke me up. I didn't dare go back to sleep.[5]

Tim drew his dream. First, he found a way to make himself safe in the drawing before interacting with the scary robot. Second, he closed his eyes, stepped back into the dream, and asked the robot, "What are you doing in my dream?" Here is what he found:

I drew my dream and the way I made myself safe was to draw a turn-off switch on the robot so I could get it to stop flashing. Without the juice, it couldn't yell or flash its lights. Without juice, it couldn't even move. Then I closed my eyes to step back into the dream. Then I asked, "What are you doing in my dream?" And the robot said, "I just want you to play ball." I said, "If you want me to play ball, stop yelling and chasing me. You scare me when you chase me. I wish you were a little more human." And that gave me the idea to draw him a heart. Once I got it to stop yelling, we could talk. When it talked about being a robot and all the hard work, I felt sorry and offered to help out on condition that I could play without getting scolded. My dad's inside that robot, I think. I gave him a new heart. I hope it works.[6]

Keep in mind that, although something of a parent may feed into a dream, as something of Tim's dad came into the dream robot, a dream image is never reducible to a real-life person.

Tim's dream points to the undue pressure that a parent can put on a child at times. Consistent with the theme of "child as teacher," Jung believed that a child's dream was not for the child to work on, but for the parents. Even if a child's dream does not portray the parent directly, the dream can help parents understand how they affect their child's emotional well-being.

It's Never Too Late to Draw Meaning from a Dream

Reflecting on your child's dreams serves your deepest intentions as a parent. A child's dream may still speak to a parent several years later, as it did for Sam's mom when her son ran into difficulty as a teenager. Something that occurred in the past can then provide a bridge to forward development. When he was four or five years old, Sam had a dream. Sam's mom remembers his dream in the following way:

> There was a fire in the living room. I was sitting on the steps of the stairway in the foyer that leads to our living room with Michael, my second son. Sam ran over to me; I was handing out lemonade to him and Michael.

The dream's two distinct scenes—the fire scene in the living room followed by the child who runs to his mom and the lemonade scene—are in contrast. The intensity of the first scene abruptly gives way to the nurturing second scene. Later, Sam's mom interpreted the fire to be an image for Sam's anger.

At the time of the dream, Sam was still struggling with his feelings about the birth of his younger brother, Michael. He used to hit Michael. Having been jealous of her sister growing up, Sam's mom showed Sam understanding, even while she also told him not to hit his brother. In hindsight, she saw herself as nurturing "but not helping out by setting limits. I was handing out lemonade instead of putting out the fire, which is bittersweet," she commented. Looking back at the dream, Sam's mom was filled with regrets for what she saw as a lack on her part in not setting boundaries for Sam early on.

When considering a dream of the past, you can take one more step. Closing off the exploration of the dream here may leave you with a taste of self-blame. Instead, you can use your child's dream as a frame within which to explore better ways to meet his or her emotional needs in the present. Let us imagine, for instance, that, lying down in a relaxed state, Sam's mom revisits Sam's dream in her imagination in order to explore alternative responses to the situation. What would "her dream" of Sam's dream be? She could re-envision her part in the dream to reach a more satisfying ending from her point of view. She could engage in an imaginary dialogue with Sam in the dream, or with the fire, which expresses a powerful energy in the dream. Another line of inquiry would be for her to ask, "What did Sam want when he ran over to me and how could I have responded? Can I still respond?"

Revisiting a child's dream from several years ago can produce rich insights and generate new perspectives on how to encounter the present. It is never too late to read meaning into a child's dream and gain insight into a parenting relationship.

Children's dreams show that children are affected not only by how their parents relate to them, but by how their parents relate to objects and people that are meaningful to the children, such as their friends, pets, and toys. How parents relate to the larger world, to the people on the street, and to the environment influences their children and their children's dreams as well.

Your child's dreams provide a rich source of information. Whereas some dreams reflect your love bond with your child, others, even if only occasional, remind you of your shortcomings and give you the opportunity to address them. When you make use of depictions of yourself in a child's dreams, your dreamguiding takes on a new dimension. As you guide your child in the art of dreaming, you are being guided in the art of parenting by your child's dreams.

Receptive to dreams, you and your child together open the door to and enter a new world, one of acknowledgment of your inner selves and connection with the boundless nurturing of dreams.

Looking into the clear source of the Senoi's way of the dream initially inspired me to find out how children who are untaught in the art of dreaming fared within their dreams. From there, I developed *dreamguiding*, an approach to help parents aid their children's development as dreamers that takes into account our modern psychologies. What I did not suspect was that beyond the guidance that parents using it can give to young dreamers, dreamguiding also enlivens connections within families.

TEN GUIDELINES

1. *Give your child your full attention as she or he relates a dream. If you cannot offer this, ask your child if you can receive the dream another time soon.*

2. *Record your child's dream as he or she reports it. Recording a dream as a child tells it communicates that you value both the dream and the telling.*

3. *When your child shares a dream with you, thank your child for telling you the dream.*

4. *Appreciate and acknowledge what is resourceful in your child's dream behavior.*

5. *Be mindful of your reactivity as you hear your child's dreams so that your child will not be influenced by worry or judgments from you.*

FOR DREAMING

6. *Do not press your child for dreams by constant questioning.*

7. *Set time aside to be present to your child at bedtime. Set everything else aside, including electronic and digital devices.*

8. *Whether your child awakens screaming inconsolably or looks for you in the morning still hurting from a difficult dream, remember that you are her or his first ally.*

9. *Take responsibility for your child's portrayal of your behavior in his or her dreams. If you have hurt your child's feelings in a dream, mend your bond with your child.*

10. *If you are puzzled by a dream of your child's, "carry it within yourself," because insights might come to you throughout your day.*

Introduction

1. Kilton R. Stewart, "Dream Theory in Malaya," *Complex* 6 (1951): 21–33. Paraphrase from 25.

2. Patricia L. Garfield, *Creative Dreaming* (New York: Ballantine Books, 1974), 80–117. Drawing from Kilton R. Stewart's "Dream Theory in Malaya" and from her visit to Senoi country in 1972, Garfield devotes an important part of her best-selling book to the Senoi's dream way. Her book was re-edited in 1995.

3. Stewart, "Dream Theory in Malaya," (1951).

4. Denyse Beaudet, *Encountering the Monster: Pathways in Children's Dreams* (New York: Continuum, 1990).

5. Richard Noone, with Dennis Holman, *In Search of the Dream People* (New York: Morrow, 1972), 23, 36.

6. Ibid., 88 ff.

7. Kilton R. Stewart, "Dream Theory in Malaya," in Charles T. Tart, ed., *Altered States of Consciousness* (New York: Wiley, 1969), 159–167.

8. Stewart, "Dream Theory in Malaya," (1951), 22.

9. Garfield, *Creative Dreaming*, 83–84.

10. G. William Domhoff, *The Mystique of Dreams: A Search for Utopia through Senoi Dream Theory* (Berkeley: University of California Press, 1985), 22. Domhoff criticized Stewart's article, "Dream Theory in Malaya," as going beyond the evidence supported by

Stewart's research, which was presented at the London School of
Economics in 1948 for Stewart's PhD in anthropology. Domhoff
reiterated his critical analysis of Senoi dream theory in an unpublished article: Domhoff, G. W. (2003). "Senoi Dream Theory: Myth,
Scientific Method, and the Dreamwork Movement." Retrieved
from the Internet: http://dreamresearch.net/Library/senoi.html.

11. Alexander Randall, "The Terrible Truth of the Temiar Senoi,"
Dream Network Bulletin 2(2) (1983): 1–2. Alexander Randall traveled
to Malaysia in 1982 in search of the truth about the Senoi. He
reported that the young boys who acted as his guides and translators
had not received any training in dreaming or been part of family dis-
cussions on dreams. They had heard stories from their grandparents
about dreams, but they had received no education in dreaming.

12. Marina Roseman, *Healing Sounds from the Malaysian Rainfor-
est: Temiar Music and Medicine, The Performance of Healing* (coedited
with Carol Laderman), and *Dream Songs and Healing Sounds: In the
Rainforests of Malaysia,* a Smithsonian/Folkways recording.

13. Arto Halonen, *A Dreamer and the Dreamtime* (Mandrake
Productions/Art Films Production, 1998).

14. Michael J. Harner, *The Jivaro* (Garden City, NY: Double-
day, 1972), 90–91, 136–139. The practices Harner describes are
either for the purpose of seeking visions and dreams of abundance
or for the purpose of acquiring a protective soul *(arutam)* or spirit,
also called a vision.

15. Sigmund Freud, *The Interpretation of Dreams,* trans. A. A.
Brill (London: George Allen & Unwin, 1915), 107. (Original work
published 1900.)

16. Melanie Klein, *The Psycho-analysis of Children,* 3d ed, trans.
Alix Strachey (London: Hogarth Press, 1963), 50. (Original work
published 1932.)

17. Anna Freud, "Introduction to Psychoanalysis," in *The Writ-
ings of Anna Freud,* Vol. 1, 1922–35 (New York: International Universities Press, 1974), 24.

18. Carl G. Jung, *The Structure and Dynamics of the Psyche,*
trans. R. F. C. Hull, Vol. 8 of *The Collective Works of C. G. Jung*
(New York: Pantheon Books, 1960), 52.

19. Carl G. Jung, *The Development of Personality,* trans. R. F. C. Hull, Vol. 17 of *The Collective Works of C. G. Jung* (Princeton, NJ: Princeton University Press, 1970), 45.

20. Frances G. Wickes, *The Inner World of Childhood* (Englewood Cliffs, NJ: Prentice-Hall, 1978), 273. (Original work published 1927.)

21. Jean Piaget, *Play, Dreams, and Imitation in Childhood* (New York: Norton, 1962), 210 ff. (Original work published 1946.)

22. Steven Luria Ablon and John E. Mack, "Children's Dreams Reconsidered," *Psychoanalytic Study of the Child* 35 (1980): 179–217.

23. Rudolph Ekstein, "Some Thoughts Concerning the Clinical Use of Children's Dreams," *Bulletin of the Menninger Clinic* 45 (1981): 115–124.

24. Maurice R. Green, "Clinical Significance of Children's Dreams," in Jules H. Masserman, ed., *Dream Dynamics: Scientific Proceedings of the American Academy of Psychoanalysis* (New York: Grune & Stratton, 1971), 72–94.

25. Richard M. Jones, "Discussion of Papers of David Foulkes, PhD, and Maurice R. Green, MD," in Jules H. Masserman, ed., *Dream Dynamics: Scientific Proceedings of the American Academy of Psychoanalysis* (New York: Grune & Stratton, 1971), 97.

26. Elena Goldstein Werlin, "An Experiment in Elementary Education," in Richard M. Jones, ed., *Contemporary Educational Psychology* (New York: Harper & Row, 1967), 233–253.

27. Kenneth Koch, *Wishes, Lies, and Dreams: Teaching Children to Write Poetry* (New York: Chelsea House, 1970).

28. Caroline DeClerque, "Educating Children to Use Dreams," *Sundance* 2 (1978): 62–70.

29. Janice O. Hudson and Carol O'Connor, "The PEACE Process: A Modified Senoi Technique for Children's Nightmares," *School Counselor* 28 (1981): 347–352.

30. Patricia Garfield, *Your Child's Dreams* (New York: Ballantine Books, 1984).

31. Alan Siegel and Kelly Bulkeley, *Dreamcatching: Every*

Parent's Guide to Exploring and Understanding Children's Dreams and Nightmares (New York: Three Rivers Press, 1998).

Chapter One

1. In H. Huon, "Physiologie du sommeil de l'enfant [Physiology of Children's Sleep]," *Revue de neuropsychiatrie infantile et d'hygiène mentale de l'enfance* 20 (1972): 815–827.

2. Eugene Aserinsky and Nathaniel Kleitman, "Two Types of Ocular Motility Occurring in Sleep," *Journal of Applied Physiology of Sleep* 8 (1955a): 8–10.

3. Eugene Aserinsky and Nathaniel Kleitman, "A Motility Cycle in Sleeping Infants as Manifested by Ocular and Gross Body Activity," *Journal of Applied Physiology of Sleep* 8 (1955b): 11–18.

4. The following diagram from http://en.wikipwdia.org/wiki/Sleep illustrates a sleep cycle including the four stages of non-REM sleep and REM sleep:

Stages 1 > 2 > 3 > 4 > 3 > 2 > REM.

A sleep cycle proceeds from the lightest sleep (1) to the deepest sleep (4), and then in reverse back to lightest sleep again. Before the discovery of REM sleep, the last stage of a sleep cycle was known as Stage 1. Since that discovery, however, the last stage of a sleep cycle came to be known as REM, and the preceding stages as NREM stages, labeled N1 to N4.

5. William C. Dement and Nathaniel Kleitman, "The Relation of Eye Movement during Sleep to Dream Activity: An Objective Method for the Study of Dreaming," *Journal of Experimental Psychology* 53 (1957): 339–346.

6. Howard P. Roffwarg, Joseph N. Muzio, and William C. Dement, "Ontogenic Development of the Human Sleep-Dream Cycle," *Science* 152 (1966): 604–619. These authors' observations of premature infants suggest that an infant born prematurely at thirty weeks spends 80 percent of his or her total sleep in REM sleep. This percentage goes down to 67 percent between thirty and thirty-five weeks and reaches 58 percent at thirty-six weeks.

7. Howard P. Roffwarg, William C. Dement, and Charles Fisher, "Preliminary Observations of the Sleep-Dream Pattern in

Neonates, Infants, Children, and Adults," in E. Harms, ed., *Problems of Sleep and Dreams in Childhood,* International Series of Monographs on Child Psychiatry (New York: Macmillan, 1964), 60–72.

8. Ibid.

9. Louis Breger, "Function of Dreams," *Journal of Abnormal Psychology Monograph* 72 (1967): 1–28.

10. Jean Piaget, *Play, Dreams, and Imitation in Childhood* (New York: Norton, 1962), 176–177. (Original work published 1946.)

11. Hermine von Hug-Hellmuth, *A Study of the Mental Life of the Child,* trans. James J. Putnam and Mabel Stevens (Washington, DC: Nervous and Mental Diseases Publishing, 1919).

12. Milton H. Erickson, "On the Possible Occurrence of a Dream in an Eight-Month Old Infant," *Psychoanalytic Quarterly* 10 (1941): 382–384.

13. Aserinsky and Kleitman, 1955b.

14. Susan Isaacs, *The Nursery Years* (New York: Vanguard Press, 1932), 96.

15. Selma H. Fraiberg, "Sleep Disturbances of Early Childhood," *Psychoanalytic Study of the Child* 5 (1950): 286.

16. John E. Mack, "Nightmares, Conflicts, and Ego Development in Childhood," *International Journal of Psychoanalysis* 46 (1965): 403–428.

17. Piaget, *Play, Dreams, and Imitation in Childhood,* 177.

18. Alan Siegel and Kelly Bulkeley, *Dreamcatching: Every Parent's Guide to Exploring and Understanding Children's Dreams and Nightmares* (New York: Three Rivers Press, 1998), 62.

19. David Foulkes, "Longitudinal Studies of Dreams in Children," in Jules H. Masserman, ed., *Dream Dynamics: Scientific Proceedings of the American Academy of Psychoanalysis* (New York: Grune & Stratton, 1971), 48–71. Foulkes noted that the dreams collected in his laboratory study of preschoolers ages three and four were relatively deficient in affective contents.

20. It is important to be aware that a dream is a subjective experience and that the object of psychology can only be the

"remembered dream." Between the moment a dream is experienced and the moment a dream is remembered, it undergoes some alterations, even in adults.

21. Mikhaëla Beaudet-DeBus, "Children's Flying Dreams," unpublished, 2001. For a science fair project at Thurgood Marshall Middle School in San Diego, 714 students from third through eighth grade filled out a questionnaire on flying dreams. The data showed that boys and girls fly higher as they grow older, symbolizing "being more independent as you grow."

Chapter Two

1. Jean Piaget, *The Child's Conception of the World,* trans. Joan and Andrew Tomlinson (Totowa, NJ: Littlefield, Adams, 1979). (Original work published 1926.) Trying to understand the stages by which children's conception of the world evolves from magical (or precausal) beliefs to concrete thinking, Piaget interviewed children on questions such as the origin of life; the origin of the sun and moon; the origin of trees, mountains, and the earth; and the origin of dreams.

2. In Sigmund Freud's theory, dreams come from the "subconscious." For Carl Jung, there is a "personal unconscious." Beyond the personal unconscious is a deeper layer of the unconscious, which Jung called the "collective unconscious." Jung also refers to the "Self," another word for soul, as the source of dreams. Some authors simply use the phrase "dream source."

3. In esoteric traditions, the solar plexus (a center situated above the navel) is sometimes understood to be a reversed brain and sometimes the heart or the center of the soul. It is also believed to be the area where the etheric body (the dream body) is attached to the physical body. When children say that they dream with their tummy, they may be sensing their solar plexus area.

4. Lilianne Lurçat, "Une approche de l'espace mental [An Approach to Mental Space]," *Journal de psychology normale et pathologique* 74 (1977): 431–449. Lurçat observed that children aged three to six draw the location of their dreams within or close

to their bodies—in the belly, the head, the eyes, or in a cartoon bubble nearby. She noted that this is not a rare phenomenon.

5. In the center of the forehead, where children commonly experience dreaming, is the center of inner vision, the pituitary, which is involved in dreaming.

6. Monique Laurendeau and Adrien Pinard, *Causal Thinking in the Child* (New York: International Universities Press, 1962), 127–128. Forty years after Piaget, two Canadian researchers, Monique Laurendeau and Adrien Pinard, repeated and standardized Piaget's study on the dream concept with a population of five hundred Québécois children aged four to twelve, with fifty children in each group. Piaget believed that the child first discovers the internal character of the origin of dreams, then of the location of the dream. Laurendeau and Pinard showed that the sequences are varied. Children begin to grasp the inner nature of the origin of dreams or of their location, but usually not both at first.

Chapter Four

1. Alan Siegel and Kelly Bulkeley, *Dreamcatching: Every Parent's Guide to Exploring and Understanding Children's Dreams and Nightmares* (New York: Three Rivers Press, 1998), 32–34.

2. David Foulkes, *Children's Dreaming and the Development of Consciousness* (Cambridge, MA: Harvard University Press, 1999), 81.

3. Ann Sayre Wiseman, *Nightmare Help: A Guide for Parents and Teachers* (Berkeley, CA: Ten Speed Press, 1989), 54–56.

Chapter Five

1. Myla and Jon Kabat-Zinn, *Everyday Blessings: The Inner Work of Mindful Parenting* (New York: Hyperion, 1997), 209.

2. "Ten Simple Ways to Trouble-Proof Your Adolescent," reprinted from the National PTA magazine in *Stampede* 2 (December 1999): 2.

3. Clarissa Pinkola Estés, *Women Who Run with the Wolves: Myths and Stories of the Wild Woman Archetype* (New York: Ballantine Books, 1992), 75–80.

4. Tomie DePaola, *The Legend of the Bluebonnet: An Old Tale of Texas* (New York: Putnam, 1983).

5. Frances Hodgson Burnett, *A Little Princess* (Boston: David R. Godine, 1989).

6. Nicole Gratton, *Rêves et complices: l'art de changer les cauchemars en beaux rêves* (Québec: Coffragants, 1996).

7. Joan Grant, *Winged Pharaoh* (London: Methuen, 1939), 9.

Chapter Six

1. Denyse Beaudet, *Encountering the Monster: Pathways in Children's Dreams* (New York: Continuum, 1990), 43–54.

2. Josephine C. Foster and John E. Anderson, "Unpleasant Dreams in Childhood," *Child Development* 7 (1936): 77–84.

3. Winsor McCay, *Little Nemo* (Paris: Pierre Horay, 1969).

4. Beaudet, *Encountering the Monster,* 130–135.

5. David Foulkes, "Dreams of the Male Child: Four Case Studies," *Journal of Child Psychology and Psychiatry* 8 (1967): 81–98.

6. David Foulkes, "Longitudinal Studies of Dreams in Children," in Jules H. Masserman, ed., *Dream Dynamics: Scientific Proceedings of the American Academy of Psychoanalysis* (New York: Grune & Stratton, 1971), 48–71.

Chapter Seven

1. Denyse Beaudet, *Encountering the Monster: Pathways in Children's Dreams* (New York: Continuum, 1990), 25–28.

2. Robert Moss, *Conscious Dreaming: A Spiritual Path for Everyday Life* (New York: Crown Trade Paperbacks, 1996), 71.

3. Beaudet, *Encountering the Monster,* 28.

Chapter Nine

1. Patricia L. Garfield, *Creative Dreaming* (New York: Ballantine Books, 1974), 89.

2. Hal Edward Runkel, *Screamfree Parenting: The Revolutionary Approch to Raising Your Kids by Keeping Your Cool* (New York: Broadway, 2007), 5–6, 31–32.

3. Ann Sayre Wiseman, *Nightmare Help: A Guide for Parents and Teachers* (Berkeley, CA: Ten Speed Press, 1989), 48–49.

4. Alan Siegel and Kelly Bulkeley, *Dreamcatching: Every Parent's Guide to Exploring and Understanding Children's Dreams and Nightmares* (New York: Three Rivers Press, 1998), 56.

5. Wiseman, *Nightmare Help,* 38.

6. Ibid., 38–39.

Index

ABOUT THE AUTHOR

Denyse Beaudet, PhD, has been a researcher and lecturer in the fields of developmental psychology and children's dreams for thirty years. She began her career as a kindergarten teacher in Canada and in France, going on to teach creativity and child development at Laval University in Québec City. Her fascination with the imaginative life of children led her to the world of children's dreams.

She is the author of *Encountering the Monster: Pathways in Children's Dreams.* She is a parent and lives with her husband in San Diego.

Hampton Roads Publishing Company

... for the evolving human spirit

HAMPTON ROADS PUBLISHING COMPANY publishes books
on a variety of subjects, including spirituality,
health, and other related topics.

For a copy of our latest trade catalog, call toll-free,
800-766-8009, or send your name and address to:

HAMPTON ROADS PUBLISHING COMPANY, INC.
1125 STONEY RIDGE ROAD • CHARLOTTESVILLE, VA 22902
e-mail: hrpc@hrpub.com • www.hrpub.com